CHARM LOVE FRIENDSHIP BRACELETS

Sherri Haab

CHARM LOVE FRIENDSHIP BRACELETS

35 UNIQUE DESIGNS WITH POLYMER CLAY, MACRAMÉ, KNOTTING, AND BRAIDING

QUARRY

Quarry Books
100 Cummings Center, Suite 406L
Beverly, MA 01915

quarrybooks.com • www.craftside.net

Acknowledgments

Thank you to my editor, Joy Aquilino, for her encouragement and support; to Zac Williams, for the beautiful photos; and to the staff at Quarto Publishing Group USA for producing a beautiful book.

First published in the United States of America in 2015 by

QUARRY BOOKS, a member of

Quarto Publishing Group USA Inc.
100 Cummings Center, Suite 406-L, Beverly, Massachusetts 01915-6101
Telephone: (978) 282-9590 | Fax: (978) 283-2742
www.quarrybooks.com

Visit www.craftside.net for a behind-the-scenes peek at our crafty world!

10 9 8 7 6 5 4 3 2

ISBN: 978-1-63159-043-6

Digital edition published in 2015
eISBN: 978-1-62788-320-7

LIBRARY OF CONGRESS CATALOGING-IN-PUBLICATION DATA

Haab, Sherri.
Charm love friendship bracelets : 35 unique designs with polymer clay, macrame, knotting, and braiding / Sherri Haab.
pages cm
ISBN 978-1-63159-043-6 (paperback) — ISBN 978-1-62788-320-7 (digital edition)
1. Charm bracelets. 2. Ropework. 3. Polymer clay craft. I. Title.
TT840.R66H33 2015
739.27'8—dc23 2014049090

Design: Laura Shaw Design, Inc., lshawdesign.com
Cover Image: Zac Williams, Williams Visual. Inc. | Photography: Zac Williams, Williams Visual, Inc.
Technical Illustrations: Rebecca Chung

Printed in China

To my husband Dan,
for his love and patience all
these years. To my children,
Rachel, Michelle, and David,
for their support and
creative inspiration.

Contents

Preface

For as long as I can remember, I've been making small jewelry objects with clay. I'm in my element with clay and always have been. The first piece of jewelry I made was a pendant using Play-Doh clay when I was about six years old. I remember waiting days for the clay to dry so I could wear it. Through my teen years and into adulthood I enjoyed working with all kinds of sculpting materials, including bread dough, papier-mâché, ceramic, and pottery clay.

After discovering polymer clay, my world changed in many ways. My sister and I wrote one of the first widely distributed books on the subject, which became the catalyst that launched my career as a craft and jewelry-making book author.

It's no wonder that polymer clay is so popular. It doesn't dry out until you cure it with heat, it's easy to manipulate, and there are more techniques than you can imagine. It's a perfect medium for jewelry making, as it can take on many forms and textures. It can be fashioned to make a piece that's whimsical and full of color, or it can be made to look very sophisticated and muted like a natural stone. I truly believe that polymer clay is the most versatile material out there for crafting jewelry. Plus, you don't need special equipment or skills to make a successful piece.

After writing many jewelry-making books on various topics over the years, with most containing a lot of clay projects, it occurred to me that all of these books shared another common theme—each contained at least one project featuring knotting in one form or another. Projects included macramé, crochet, and needlework techniques. Just like my clay obsession, my love of threadwork extends back to my childhood. As a child, I remember making a beaded ring by following a pattern I had retrieved from a box of seed beads a neighbor had given to me. After threading tiny seed beads row by row according to the diagram, I became so excited to see the pattern began to emerge. Another project from the early 1970s was inspired by a ring my mother had made by crocheting metallic elastic thread and embedding a cluster of pearl beads on top. I was thrilled when she taught me how to make one of my own, and I proudly wore this treasured keepsake to elementary school. Since then, I've always been drawn to fiber jewelry and have enjoyed working with knotting techniques.

One day when I was yearning to work with polymer clay again, the thought occurred to me: why not write a book combining two of my favorite mediums—clay and thread! The more I thought about it, the more excited I became. The two mediums felt compatible to me, and it seemed only natural that there should be an entire book dedicated to the idea. In my mind, there were so many ways you could combine them with unlimited design possibilities. Ideas started pouring in.

Clay and thread go perfectly well together for many reasons. One of my favorite observations is that both mediums present color as a dynamic artistic expression. Thread and cord are available in every color imaginable. Polymer clay can be mixed to match or coordinate with any chosen thread or cord color. There are also clay and thread variations that provide similar reflective qualities. For example, metallic threads are paired with a painted clay centerpiece in the Silver Threads project on page 102. Not only do the colors match, but the silver paint and metallic threads both reflect light, delivering a subtle shimmer.

The compatibility of clay and thread makes it easy to pair clay designs or styles with meaningful knot patterns. Take, for example, Sweet Bee on page 116. For this design, I selected a golden yellow thread and used an alternating knotted pattern characteristic of a beehive or a honeycomb pattern to go with a vintage bee illustration.

A knotted pattern can enhance a polymer clay design to interpret a style. For example, think of a geometric bead paired with a sleek monochromatic braided cord versus a sculptured clay rose bead threaded on a multiknotted wrap bracelet design with lots of color and texture. One idea is minimalistic and modern, whereas the other has a handmade, carefree playfulness to it.

In addition to pairing style and color, clay and thread have similar tactile and weight qualities. Delicate clay pieces can be made to balance a delicate thread pattern. Sculpting your own beads allows you to control the scale and weight of a design rather than relying on what is available with purchased beads.

With so many options, there is lots of room for creativity. The projects in this book vary in material and style, so you will be sure to find something that speaks to you and is fun to make. A quick trip to the craft supply store and you will find everything you need to get started. Enjoy the projects!

CHAPTER ONE

POLYMER CLAY ESSENTIALS

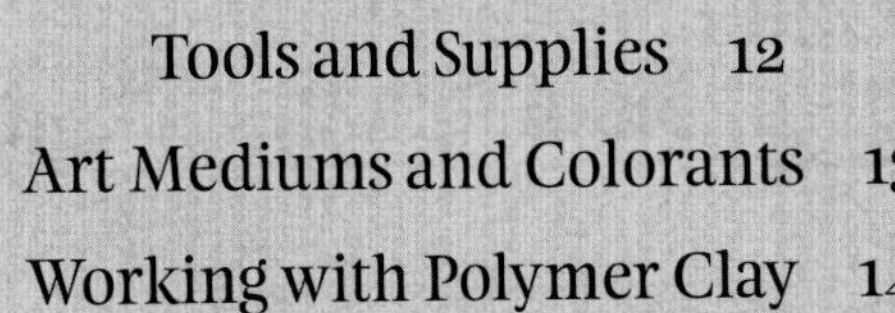

Polymer clay is sold at arts and craft stores in a variety of colors and forms through several manufacturers. There are many different varieties of clay, including solid opaque, translucent, glitter-infused, glow-in-the-dark, and neon, just to name a few. Clay is also available in liquid form with companion products such as varnish and adhesives that are made specifically for the clay.

Solid blocks of colored polymer clay are the most common type available. Some varieties are softer than others and better suited for sculpting, whereas others are better for shaping geometric beads and creating caned designs. Polymer clay is baked at a low temperature to cure into a permanent form.

Translucent clay resembles frosted glass when cured. Inks, pigments, and paints can be mixed into the clay to tint it with color.

Liquid polymer clay is a versatile material. It can be baked as is to create thin pieces that you can almost see through. Or you can use it as a glossy coating by baking it over regular polymer clay. A variety of mediums can be added to change the texture or color of the liquid polymer. It can also be used as a means to adhere pieces of clay through baking.

Tools and Supplies

Working with polymer clay is easiest if you've gathered a few essential tools beforehand. Here's a general list of what you may need, but be sure to check the materials list for additional supplies specific to each project.

- Sheet of **plastic, glass, or waxed paper** to protect your work surface
- **Roller or pasta roller** for rolling sheets of clay
- Variety of small **clay or cookie cutters** available from craft and cake decorating supply stores
- **Rubber stamps**
- **Molds** to texture and mold clay—you can purchase molds or make your own.
- **Leather stamping tools** to make lovely patterned textures on clay
- **Clay sculpting tools**, such as those used for ceramics, for adding details or making attachments
- **Polymer clay sculpting tools**, available through craft stories—ordinary items you might find in the kitchen or sewing room work well too.
- **Mat cutter blade**, **craft knife**, or ordinary **kitchen knife**
- Handheld **pin vise drill** with drill bit to enlarge holes in cured polymer clay beads
- Small **toaster oven** and a small **baking tray** dedicated for polymer clay work
- Oven **thermometer**
- **Heavier gauged wire** for baking beads, available in the floral department of many craft stores—these wires are heavier gauged than wire found in the beading section.

- **Heat embossing tool** for baking or curing liquid polymer onto clay beads—the tool will get as hot as an oven, so take care not to burn the clay or anything else while using it. Don't use an industrial heat gun that you might find at a hardware store, as these are extremely hot and are not meant for craft applications.
- **Plastic-coated wire**, commonly referred to as telephone wire, for fashioning into loops to be embedded and baked into polymer clay—the plastic coating compliments the texture and color of polymer clay. If plastic-coated wire is not available, use metal wire instead.

Art Mediums and Colorants

A variety of different effects can be achieved by applying paint, varnish, or ink to polymer clay. You can also change the texture with glitter, beads, or powders.

Acrylic paint works well with polymer clay. Brush it over baked clay to bring out the details of a texture or use it to tint unbaked translucent clay.

Antiquing paint or gel conveys a vintage look to baked clay charms. Paint it over cured clay and then rub if off, leaving it in the recessed textures of a pattern.

Colored pencils of good quality can be used to decorate the surface of baked clay.

Glitter and glass beads can be embedded into clay to add interest and texture. Be sure to use glitter or beads made of a heatproof material such as glass.

Pigment powders can be applied to the surface of baked or unbaked clay to change the color or sheen of a textured surface.

Gilders paste is a wax that can be rubbed over baked textures on the clay to highlight the design. The paste is available in metallic as well as solid matte colors.

Gloss and matte varnishes will add shine or protective coatings to baked clay surfaces. Make sure the product you are using is compatible with polymer clay. Some will react with clay, becoming tacky, or they may begin to delaminate over time.

Alcohol-based inks contain strong pigments to add rich color to the surface or when kneaded into clay.

Sand, embossing powders, and foils can be used to create special effects such as faux stone, concrete, and metal.

Working with Polymer Clay

This section offers guidelines for safely handling and successfully mixing and finishing polymer clay.

ESSENTIAL SAFETY TIPS

Always cure your polymer clay charms and beads according to the manufacturer's recommended temperatures and times. (For additional safety information, request the Material Safety Data Sheet, or the MSDS, from the manufacturer.) Polymer clay will produce toxic fumes if it's overheated or burned, so use a toaster oven dedicated to baking your polymer pieces. Also be sure to test the oven with an oven thermometer before baking anything to make sure the temperature is accurate, as the oven's actual temperature may be hotter than its setting indicates. Always preheat any oven you're using to cure clay.

Always wash your hands after working with polymer clay, especially before eating.

Never use tools that you've used with polymer clay to prepare food.

Always handle sharp blades, tools, or knives extremely carefully.

WORK SURFACES

Work on a nonstick surface such as a piece of waxed paper or a glass or ceramic tile with a smooth surface. Don't use surfaces that you use for food preparation or that the clay might react with or stain, such as certain countertop materials. Waxed paper is an ideal working surface because clay won't stick to it and it's disposable. (It's also a great surface for mixing paint and epoxy resin.)

CLEANING UP

Use baby wipes or rubbing alcohol to clean stubborn clay residue from your hands. Clean the clay off your hands after working with one color and before working with another. You can use wipes and alcohol to remove residue from tools and surfaces as well.

CONDITIONING

The process of conditioning polymer clay—kneading it to evenly distribute the plasticizers and make the clay body more consistent, allowing it to cure into a stronger finished product—varies for different clay types. Most clays are soft and ready to use right out of the package, requiring minimal kneading before starting a project.

If your clay is a little stiff, crumbly, or hard to mold, start by warming small pieces of the clay in your hands. Or you can change the clay's consistency by adding polymer softeners. Once the clay is workable, begin to knead it, keeping it compact and dense, and it will gradually become soft and pliable. Avoid folding the clay over and over, which might trap air between the layers and create bubbles that will remain even after curing. If you do see bubbles in a piece prior to curing it, pierce them with a needle or needle tool to release the air. You can also condition clay by running it through a pasta roller, which can be especially helpful when working with large quantities.

COLOR MIXING

You can mix a wide range of custom colors by using just **the three primaries—red, yellow, and blue.** A color can also be altered by adding white, black, or another color.

Mixing two or more clays together very thoroughly will yield a single, solid hue; you'll get a nice marbled effect if you knead them together without mixing them completely. Marbling can be subtle or bold, depending on the colors you're combining.

① To create a **tint**—a light value of a color—add white to the original color until the desired value is achieved. If the color you're aiming for is very light, as with the light blue shown here, you may want to start with white and add small amounts of the darker color, as its pigment may be overpowering.

② To create **a secondary color—green, orange, and purple**—add two primary colors together. Adding a little yellow to blue creates a medium blue-green.

③ In this example of creating a secondary by mixing two primaries, adding red to blue yields violet.

④ To tone down or neutralize a color, add its **complement** to it. Complementary colors are those that lie opposite one another on a color wheel. For example, adding orange to a dark blue will create a neutral gray-blue.

①

②

③

④

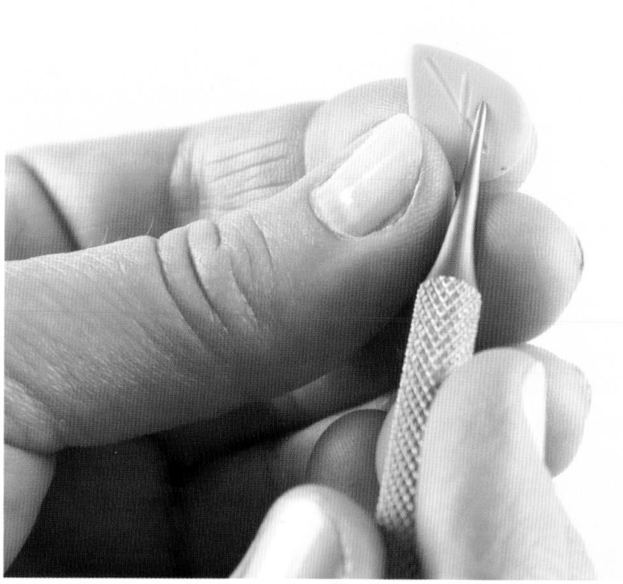

SCULPTING

After conditioning, polymer clay is ready to shape or mold into beads or figures. For rolling bead shapes or sculpting tiny elements, your hands are often the best tools. A simple round bead can be rolled between the palms of your hands. Ropes or snakes of clay are easiest to roll on a flat surface using your hand to apply pressure while rolling to lengthen and thin the rope of clay.

Use a toothpick or ceramic sculpting tools to shape more complex forms with the clay. Clay will stick to itself as long as you blend the pieces together with a tool. Smooth one piece of clay into another by working the edges together or use a product designed to adhere polymer clay pieces. Previously baked or broken polymer pieces can also be joined and re-baked using these methods.

ROLLING SHEETS

Work on a protective surface such as waxed paper to roll sheets of polymer clay. An acrylic roller or brayer works well for rolling out the clay. You can also use a smooth drinking glass.

If you are rolling large sheets or doing production work, use a pasta roller that is dedicated for clay use. Sheets of clay formed with a pasta roller are particularly useful for caned work where precision matters. Sheets can be rolled to specific thicknesses with the pasta roller. Pasta rollers have adjustable settings to accommodate this. Condition the clay first to soften it and then pass the clay through the top of the pasta roller as you crank the handle. To prevent the clay from jamming into the rollers, always start on the thickest setting and then roll progressively thinner sheets.

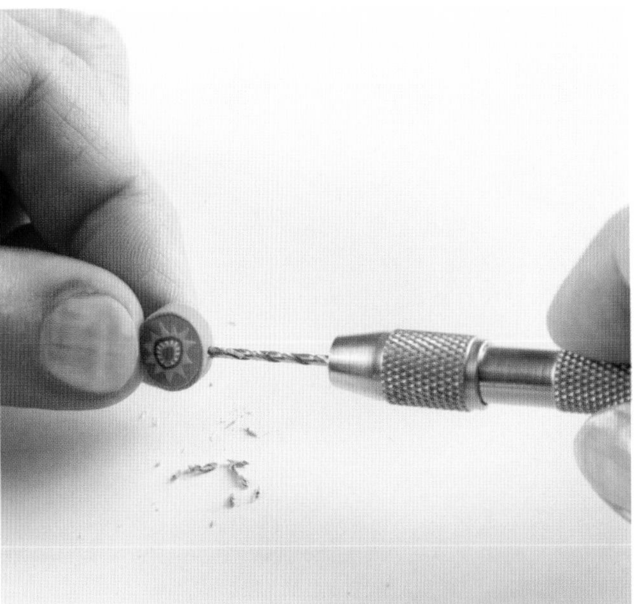

TEXTURING

Polymer clay looks great with texture added to the surface. You can texturize clay with rubber stamps, leather stamping tools, found objects, lace, fabric, seashells, and other items. Almost anything that has a relief pattern is fair game.

If you are using a rubber stamp to texture clay, it is usually easiest to press the clay onto the stamp, especially if the stamp is larger than the small piece of clay you are using. This method allows you to feel how deep the texture is pressed into the clay and to control the thickness of the clay. Dust the rubber stamp with a layer of talcum powder or cornstarch to prevent the clay from sticking. With smaller stamping implements like leather stamping tools, it works well to stamp directly over and onto a sheet or ball of clay until you are pleased with the depth.

After adding texture, bring out the details by applying pigment powders, gilders paste, colored pencil, or acrylic paints to the surface either before or after baking, depending on the medium.

MAKING BEADS

Beads can be made by rolling by hand or cutting shapes with tools. After forming a bead, let it rest or cool it in the refrigerator before piercing so it will hold its shape. To pierce a bead, use a needle tool to go through one side of the bead about half way and then turn the bead around and pierce back through from the opposite side. There will be more distortion if you only pierce from one direction.

If you want a larger hole in the bead than what your piercing tool allows, enlarge the hole after baking using a pin vise with a drill bit as described below. It is difficult to make a large hole in an unbaked clay bead without ruining the shape.

After baking the beads you can drill larger holes if desired. To drill through a bead, use a pin vise fitted with the appropriate sized drill bit and twist the bit into the baked clay bead. Go through one side of the bead and then drill back through the other side until shavings clear out of the hole. Drilling through polymer clay should always be done by hand using a hand drill or pin vise. NOTE: Do not use an electric drill as the plastic will melt on your drill bit.

Alter baked beads by sanding, carving, painting, or applying other mediums to the surface. If you use a coating such as a polymer lacquer, it helps to suspend the beads on a wire while the lacquer dries.

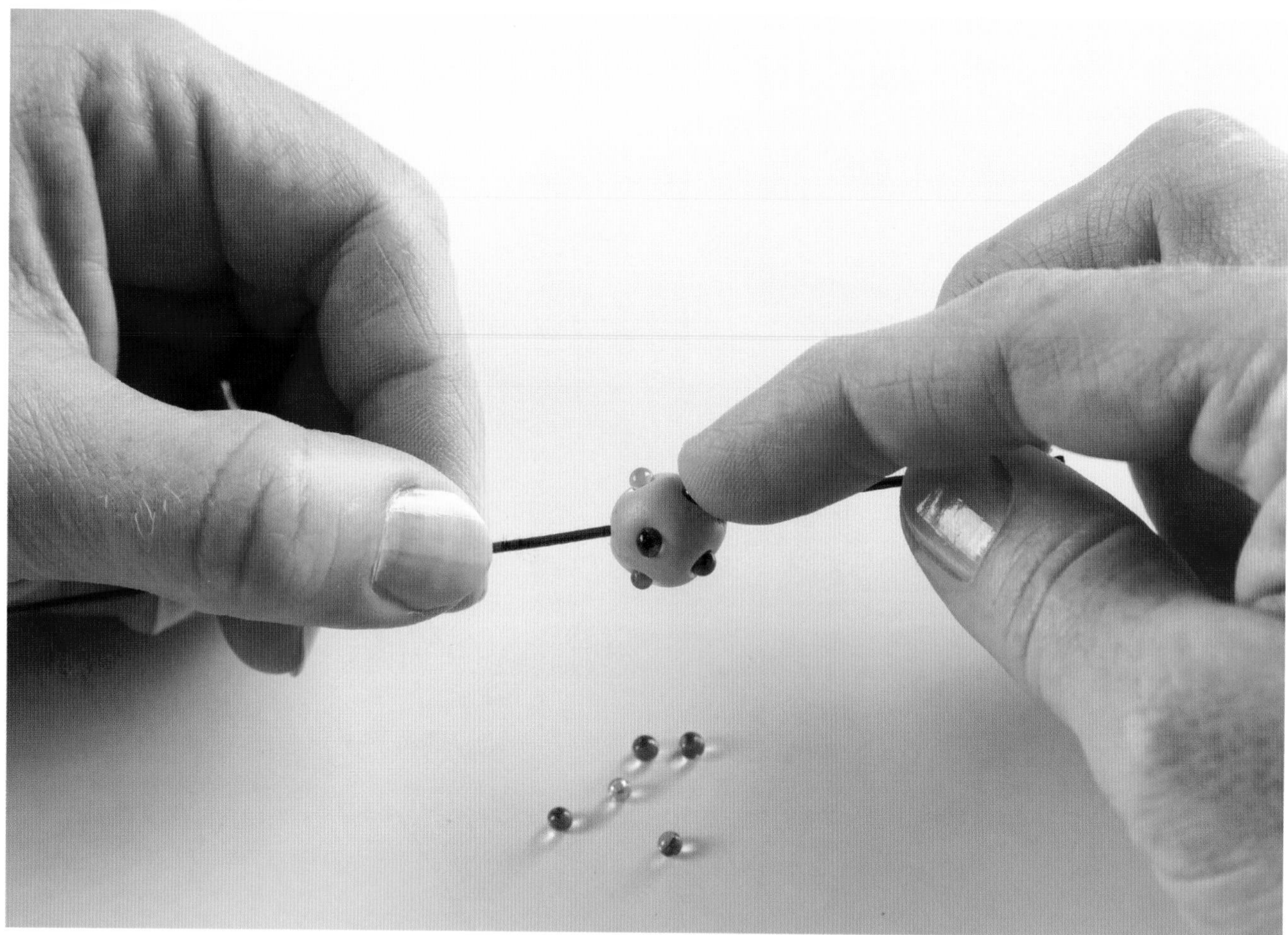

EMBEDDING AND MIX-INS

Ovenproof materials can be mixed into polymer clay prior to baking to add interesting elements or textures to the clay. Embed wire or other jewelry findings into the clay for functional purposes.

If you are adding rhinestones or beads, use glass instead of plastic. Some plastics melt or emit harmful fumes. To embed a stone or bead, push it deeply into the clay. Shape the clay around and slightly over the edges of the stone to ensure that it stays in place. If the stone is loose after baking, use a two-part epoxy resin to affix the stone.

Sand, glitter, and embossing powders add textures that resemble stone or granite after the clay is baked. Knead small amounts of these mediums into the clay to evenly distribute them and then bake the clay.

When embedding wire or other findings into clay, a twist, bend, or notch in the wire or finding will help anchor it into the clay. To secure a wire loop, for example, twist the end of the wire at the base of the loop and bury it into the clay, pushing the clay in around the sides. Plastic-coated wires work best, as the plastic tends to fuse a bit with the clay. Metal wire and findings need to be embedded deeply into the clay, with a little bit of clay built up around them to prevent the metal from pulling out after baking. It helps to patch a piece of clay over the base of a wire loop prior to baking to keep it embedded. Test the wire or finding after baking to make sure it is secure. If not, pull out the wire or finding and apply quick-setting epoxy resin before replacing it into the baked clay. Let the epoxy cure.

MAKING MOLDS

To make polymer clay charms from an old button or keepsake, create a mold of the button and then cast multiple charms from it. You can even sculpt an original design from polymer clay to mold.

Silicone mold putty is now available in craft stores, and it is the perfect material for mold making. It is a two-part putty that becomes a solid rubber material after mixing the two components. The result is a flexible mold for casting. It does not require a release agent, as the rubber will not stick to most surfaces.

Making a Silicone Mold

Step 1: Knead equal parts of each component of two-part silicone mold putty until the putty is uniform in color.

Step 2: Form into a ball and flatten on a smooth, nonstick surface like waxed paper. Press the object you wish to mold face down into the putty, making sure the putty surrounds the object around all sides.

Step 3: Let the putty set up with object in place. The putty has cured if when you press on it with your fingernail it bounces back without leaving an impression. The curing time varies depending on the brand you are using. After curing, remove the object.

Step 4: Press a ball of conditioned polymer clay into the mold to fill it.

Step 5: Flex the mold to release the clay. The clay should fall out of the mold easily. Bake the clay charm as desired for your finished piece. The mold can be used over an over again to make more charms.

Making a Polymer Clay Mold

A rigid mold can be made using polymer clay. Follow step 2 for Making a Silicone Mold, using polymer clay instead of the silicone putty to make the mold. Remove the object, and bake according to manufacturer's instructions. Before pressing polymer clay into the finished mold, dust the mold with cornstarch or baby powder to prevent sticking.

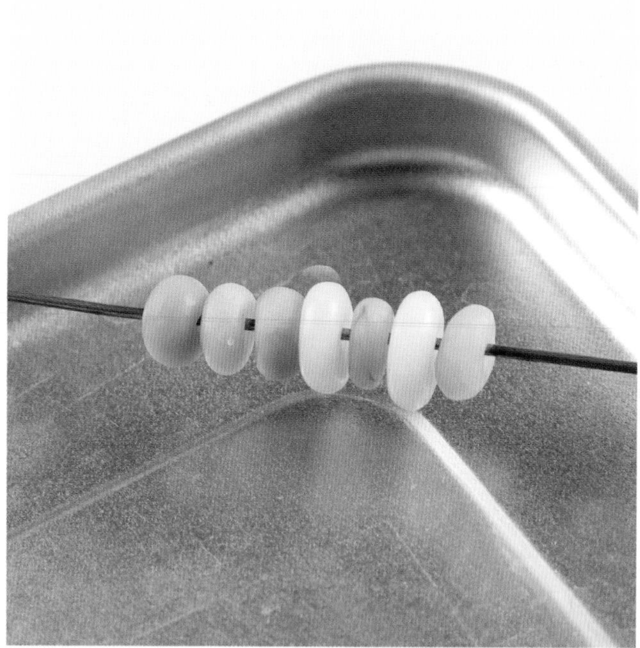

If you make round beads, you can bake them on a wire suspended over a pan. Or you may bake beads flat on a piece of plain paper or a Teflon sheet. The sheet will prevent the beads from developing a flat or shiny spot where they rest against the pan.

BAKING/CURING

Bake your clay beads and charms according to the manufacturer's instructions, as brands may vary slightly. Generally, most polymer clay types are baked at 275°F (135°C, or gas mark 1) for about 30 minutes. Liquid and translucent types vary and some can be cured with an embossing heat tool commonly used with embossing powders for rubber stamps.

Use the baking tray that comes with the toaster oven or, if using a regular oven, use a glass or metal baking pan. Line pans with a piece of paper or other non-stick liner to prevent pieces from developing a shiny spot on the bottom and from sticking to the pan.

Always set a timer and make sure the temperature of your oven is accurate. Some colors turn dark when they are baked for a long time. You can brighten the clay by adding white clay to the original color mix to compensate for shifts in darkness due to baking.

Pieces can be left in the oven to cool after you turn it off or removed and left to cool at room temperature. Always use hot pads when removing pans and carefully handle clay pieces just removed from the oven, as they can be very hot.

FINISHING TECHNIQUES AND MEDIUMS

After baking your pieces, there are a number of surface treatment options that can be utilized to alter the surface of polymer clay. Consider using acrylic paints, antiquing mediums, colored pencils, gilders paste, liquid polymer clay products, or varnishes to achieve a variety of different looks.

To add more color to the surface of baked clay, use acrylic paints. Brush the paint over the texture of a baked clay piece and then wipe the paint off of the raised areas, leaving paint in the recessed areas. Or simply paint the surfaces without wiping off the excess. Once the paint is dry, seal the paint with a coating made especially for polymer clay.

Antiquing mediums are acrylic products that are easier to wipe off than paints. You can mix your own by adding acrylic paint to antiquing medium or you can buy premixed versions at the craft store. Use antiquing medium in the same way as acrylic paint and then use a paper towel to wipe off the excess, leaving antique finish in the recessed areas. Seal with varnish to protect the finish.

To add color with pencils, buy good quality pencils from an art supply store. The better brands have richer pigments in them and the color will be more intense. Rub colored pencil over baked clay to add another layer of color and bring out textures in the clay. Seal the pencil markings with a polymer varnish coating to protect it.

Gilders paste is a rub-on product that is available at art supply stores or from furniture refinishing suppliers. Simply rub the paste over the clay to highlight textures or edges of baked clay. Buff it with a soft cloth for a soft sheen. Pigment powders provide a similar finish and are best used before baking so that the powder will stick to the clay. Seal with a polymer varnish coating after baking.

Liquid polymer clay products will provide a glasslike coating when baked over previously baked polymer clay pieces. Brush clear liquid polymer over a bead and then

Above are versions of a clay button with different surface treatments. Top row, from left to right: gilders paste (shown on translucent clay), white acrylic paint, pink colored pencil, German silver metallic wax; bottom row, from left to right: antiquing gel, liquid polymer with alcohol ink, yellow acrylic paint, and antiquing gel (shown on translucent clay).

bake it in an oven or use a rubber stamp embossing heat tool according to the clay manufacturer's instructions. If you want color, some liquid polymers are sold with color mixed in, or you can tint the polymer yourself. To tint liquid polymer, use a toothpick to mix a little acrylic paint or alcohol ink with the polymer on a piece of waxed paper. Paint the colorful liquid over the baked piece and then bake again for a ceramic glaze look.

Polymer clay manufacturers also offer coatings such as varnishes to seal the surface of the clay to protect paints, powders, or to add shine. Check the bottle to determine whether the finish is matte or gloss. The coatings are usually cured by air-drying, with no baking required. Since polymer will react with acrylics over time, it is wise to use a coating made specifically for polymer clay. You might end up with tacky surfaces on your beads months or even years down the line if you use the wrong product.

CHAPTER TWO

KNOTTING AND JEWELRY-MAKING BASICS

Knotting Materials and Tools

Almost any type of cord or heavy thread can be used to make friendship bracelets. You'll need only a few tools and supplies to make the knotting process easier.

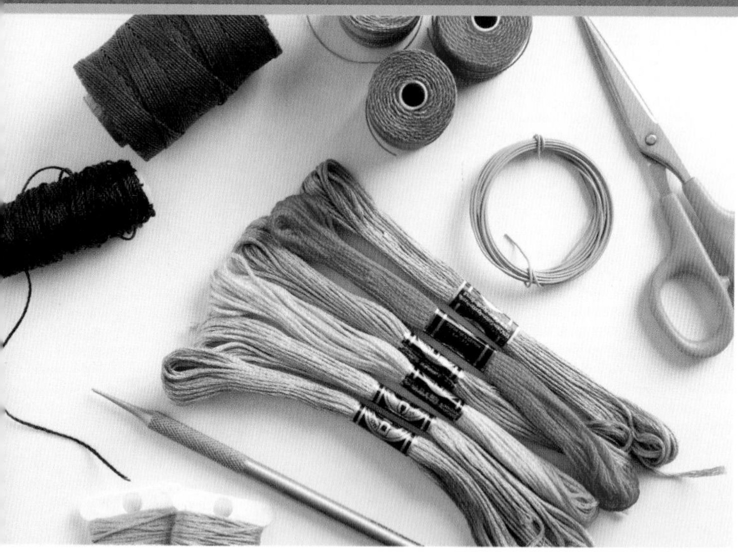

THREADS AND CORDS

Traditional bracelets are made using **embroidery thread,** which is inexpensive and manufactured in hundreds of colors. It is widely available from craft and fabric stores.

Waxed cotton and linen cord both offer several beneficial traits for knotting. They have a warm organic feel. These natural materials often have a wax coating on the cord which keeps it stiff, making it easier to thread and knot. It also adds structure to the finished bracelet.

Twisted nylon cord is commonly used for beading and macramé. It is sold in bead shops in a variety of colors and is available in different thicknesses. This cord doesn't stretch or fray easily, and the ends can be finished with heat to melt the nylon, which will prevent fraying. Fine twisted nylon cord will fit through small beads, making it a good choice for projects where bead hole size is an issue. Look for the standard weight, commonly referred to as #18, which is the size used for most of the projects using nylon cord in this book. Thicker and finer cords are also available.

Fine leather cord, Chinese knotting cord, metallic thread, hemp, and **ribbon** are other suitable options for knotting bracelets.

BASIC TOOLS

The great thing about friendship bracelets is that they don't require many tools aside from your own two hands. You will need these tools for working with threads and cords.

Sharp scissors for cutting.

A pair of fingernail clippers will serve as a clever substitute for those on the go and are especially helpful for air travel, when sharp objects aren't allowed.

A **clipboard,** which can be purchased from an office supply store, is handy for anchoring or holding threads and provides an easy work surface that's portable.

Use a **small piece of fine wire** bent in half for stringing thread through beads.

Small beading needles are also good to have on hand for delicate seed beads or threads.

Use **tape** to hold core threads taut as you tie knots.

A **needle tool** is useful for unpicking knots in thread when you make a mistake.

Essential Knotting Techniques

This section explains and illustrates the knotting techniques that are used to create the bracelet designs in this book. Use these instructions to practice your knotting skills before you start your first project. Throughout this section and in the project instructions, the thread that's used to tie the knots is called the *knotting thread* and the thread on which knots are tied is called the *core thread*.

OVERHAND KNOT

This is the knot used to secure threads together before beginning a knot pattern or to finish off the ends.

To tie the knot, make a loop with one thread (or a group of threads) and bring the end of the thread(s) through the loop, pulling tight.

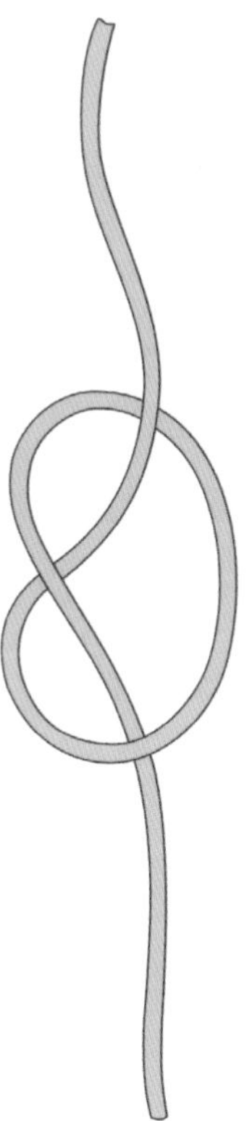

THREE-STRAND BRAID

A braid creates a pattern by weaving threads together rather than knotting them. You can use single threads or multiple fibers divided into three sections. Chain can also be woven into the pattern alongside one of the threads.

Step 1: To weave a braid with three threads, tie three threads together at one end using an overhand knot and pull them down next to each other. Bring the left thread (blue) over the center thread (green); this thread (blue) now becomes the center.

Step 2: Bring the right thread (yellow) over the center thread (blue); now the yellow thread becomes the center. To proceed, bring the green thread over the yellow. Repeat the pattern by alternating left and right threads, each time crossing over the center thread to form the braid.

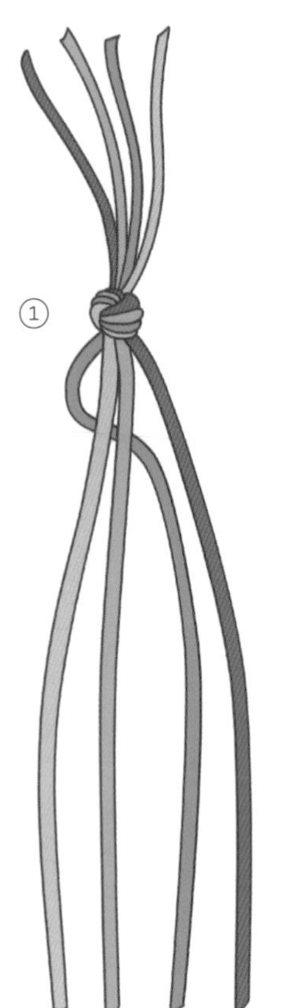

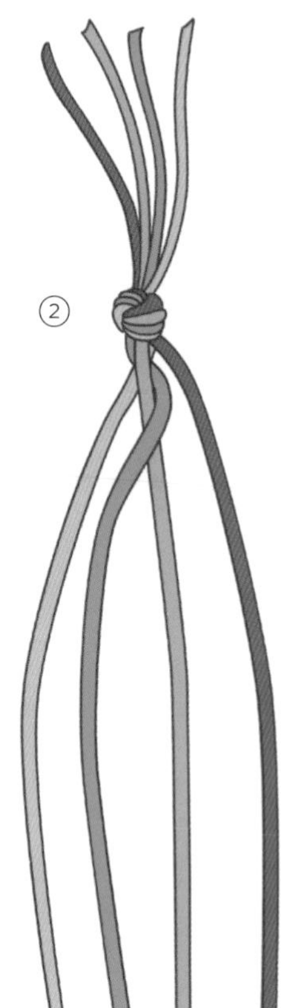

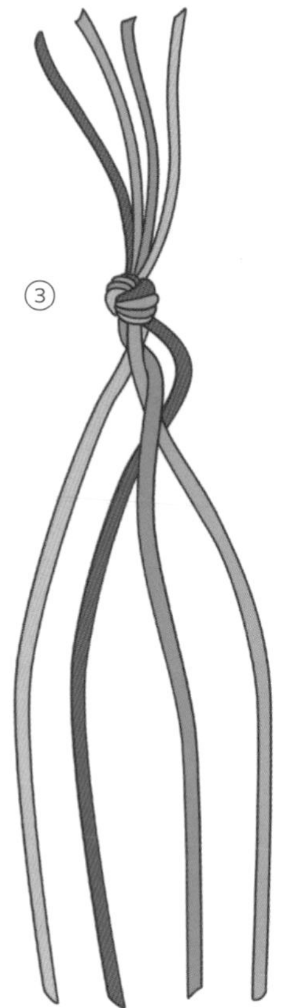

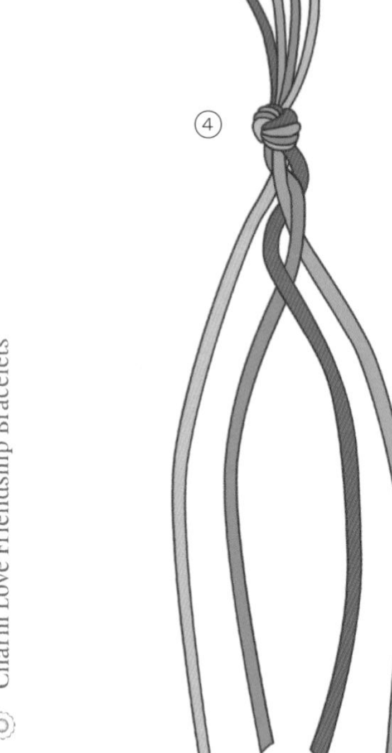

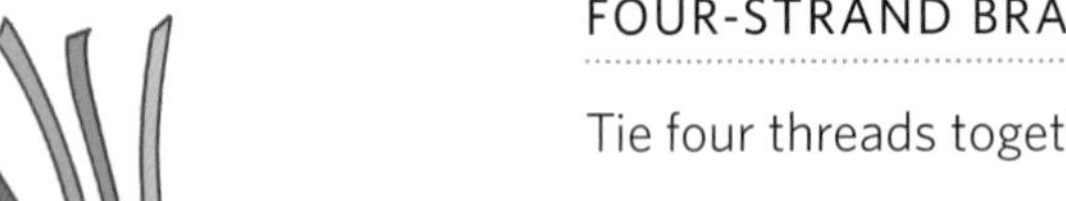

FOUR-STRAND BRAID

Tie four threads together at one end using an overhand knot.

Step 1: Pull the blue thread behind the two threads in the middle (yellow and green).

Step 2: Bring the same blue thread back over the green thread, placing it between the yellow and green threads (with the yellow on the left and the green on the right).

Step 3: From the right side, pull the purple thread behind the two center threads.

Step 4: Bring the same (purple) thread back over the blue thread, placing it between the blue and green threads, pulling all threads taut to tighten as you go. Continue the pattern by alternating sides, wrapping behind the center two threads and then around to the center of those same threads each time.

HALF KNOT

This knot is formed with four threads. Tie them together on one end using an overhand knot.

Step 1: Pull two of the (blue) threads straight down to serve as the center core. Place the other two cords out to each side (yellow on the left and green on the right).

Step 2: To tie the half knot, bring the (yellow) thread from the left and pull it over the two (blue) core threads to form a number 4.

Step 3: Pick up the (green) thread from the right and pass it over the tail of the yellow thread and then up and under the blue core threads, exiting up through the left loop as shown above. Pull both outside threads tightly while keeping the core stationary and tight.

Step 4: If you keep tying the half knot over and over, it forms a twisted pattern around the core. Flip your work over as you progress, as the twist forces you to work around to the backside of the core.

SQUARE KNOT

The square knot consists of two opposite half knots. Start with the thread on the left to tie the first half knot and begin with the thread on the right to tie the second half knot.

Step 1: To begin, tie the four threads together using the two in the center as the core. Follow the directions for the half knot to begin the first half of the knot, starting with the thread on the left as shown in the illustration for the half knot.

Step 2: Tie another half knot directly under it, but this time start with the thread on the right.

Step 3: Bring the right (yellow) thread across the two core threads to create a backwards number 4.

Step 4: Now bring the left (green) thread over the tail of the yellow thread you just pulled over from the right. Bring it under the core threads and back up through the loop on the right side. Pull both sides snug around the core.

Note: You can tie a square knot without core threads as a finish knot or to secure threads.

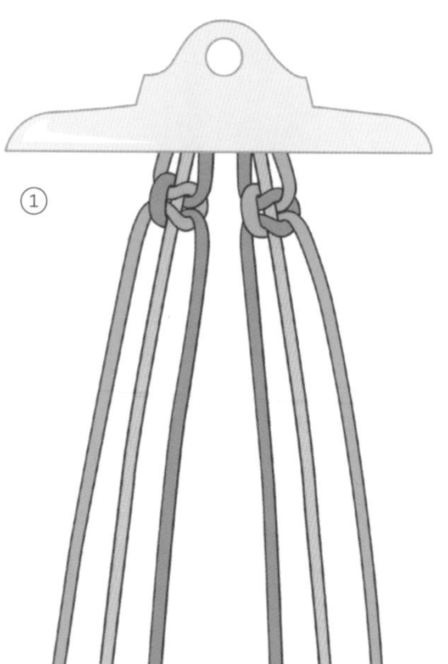

Step 1: Align six threads across your work space, matching the outside, middle, and inside thread colors as shown. Tie a square knot with the three threads on the left and another square knot with the three threads on the right.

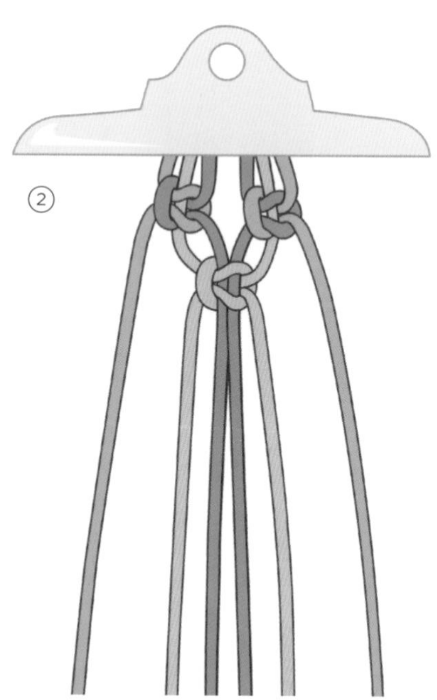

Step 2: For the next row, bring the two middle (blue) threads together to serve as the core for the next knot. Tie a square knot with the (yellow) threads over the blue core. Now you will have one square knot in the center.

ALTERNATING SQUARE KNOT

This knot uses a minimum of six threads, but you can use more to create a wider pattern. Use even numbers of threads for a neater look. This example uses three colors of thread which were doubled, giving you a total of six threads to work with. The colors can be arranged in different orders to change the overall appearance of the finished bracelet.

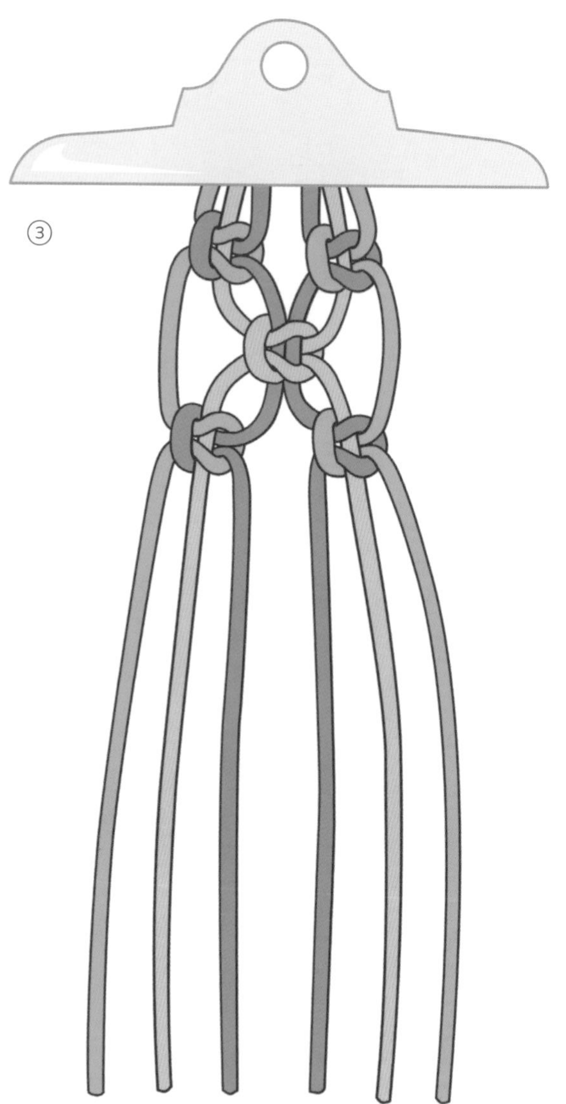

Step 3: For the third row, tie a square knot with the three threads on the left and then another square knot on the right, just as you did in step 1. Continue the pattern by alternating steps 1 and 2.

HALF-HITCH KNOT

An essential macramé knot, the half-hitch forms a spiral pattern by tying one cord or thread around another multiple times. This knot can be worked either from right to left (as shown in the main illustration) on the right or from left to right (as shown below).

Step 1: Tie two threads together on one end using an overhand knot.

Step 2: Keeping the core thread (shown at right in blue, A) straight and taut, bring the knotting thread (in green, B) to the right and loop it over and around the core, exiting to the right and pulling the knotting thread tightly around the core to finish.

Step 3: Repeat step 2 to create a spiral pattern along the length of the core thread. Note that you'll need to tie five or six knots before they begin to spiral; as you continue tying knots, you'll have to turn your work to follow the spiral's structure.

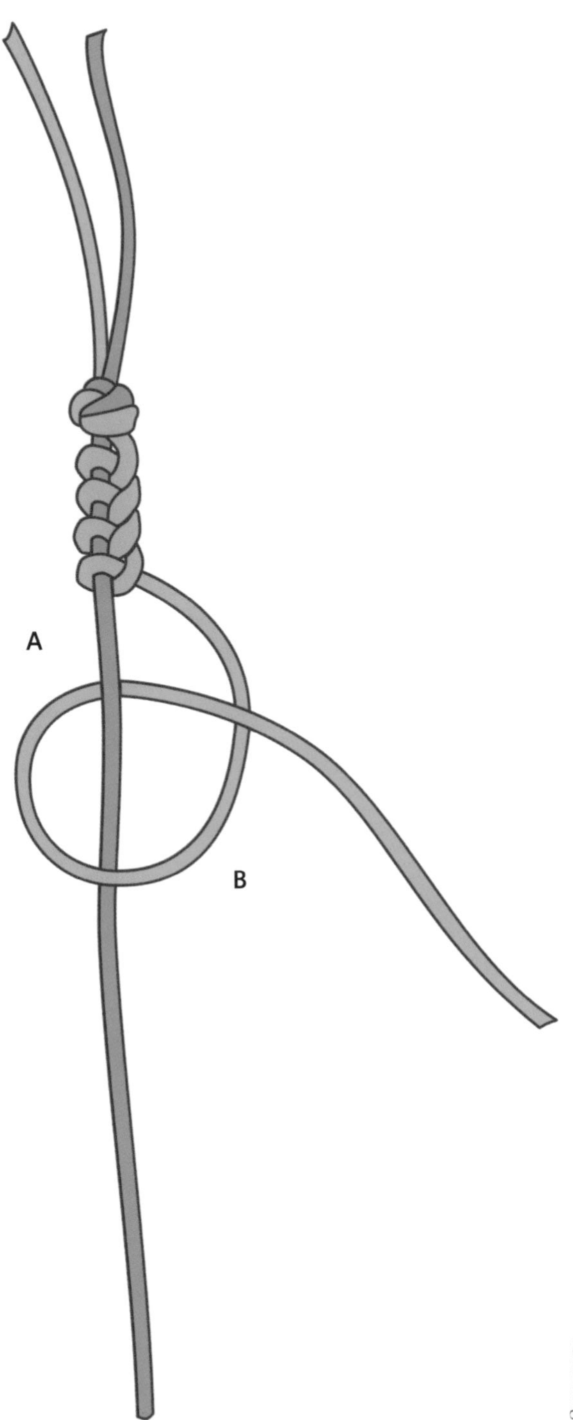

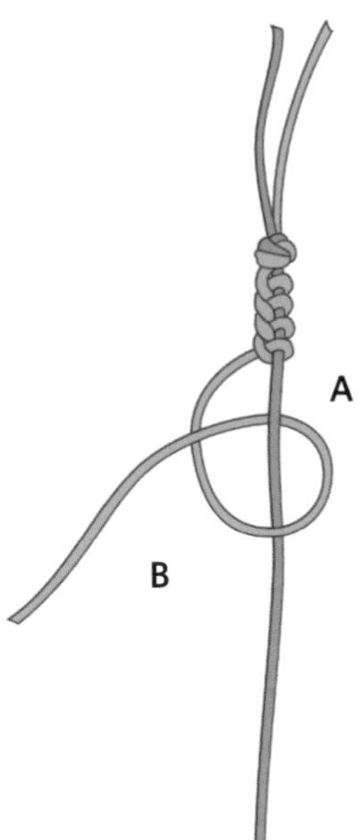

The half-hitch knot can also be worked from left to right.

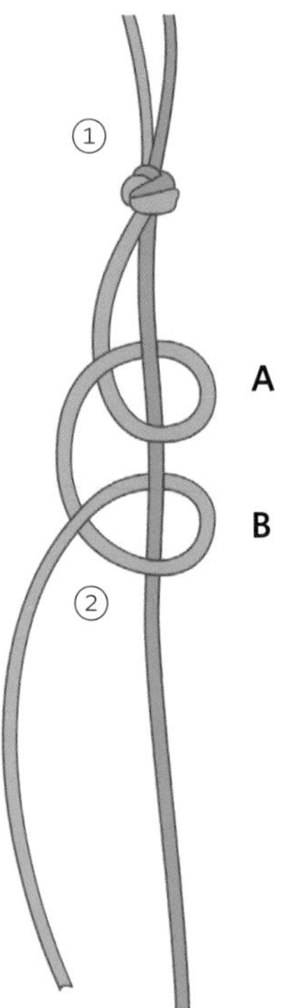

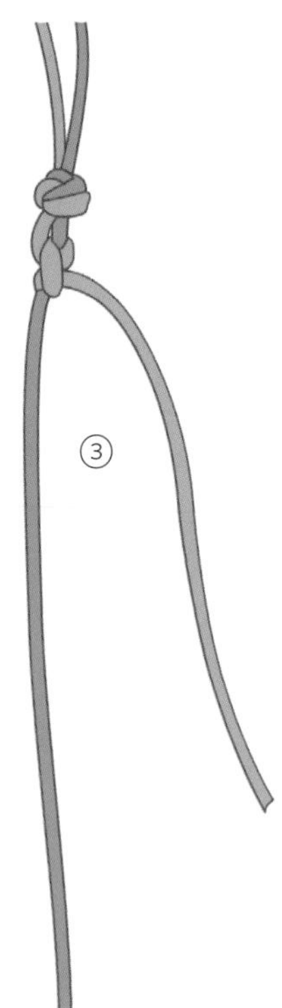

DOUBLE HALF-HITCH

The double half-hitch is the knot most commonly used to create a traditional "friendship bracelet." It can be tied from the left to the right or from the right to the left.

Step 1: Tie the two threads together at one end using an overhand knot. One thread will serve as the core while the other is used to tie the knot.

Step 2: Bring the (blue) core thread straight down and hold it taut. Bring the other thread (green) to the left side; this is the thread that will be used to tie the knot. Loop this thread over and around the blue core thread, exiting to the left as shown on the first top loop in the illustration (A). Pull the first green loop tightly around the blue core thread. Repeat the same loop again, wrapping the green thread over the blue core and through to the left as you did in step 1 (B).

Step 3: As you are pulling the thread around to finish the second loop from step 2, pull tight around the core. As you tighten down, you will pull the green thread to the right side. The knot will snap into place and the threads will switch places from where they started (see illustration). As you practice, the second loop and finished knot will be tied in one continuous motion, making a neatly formed double half-hitch knot.

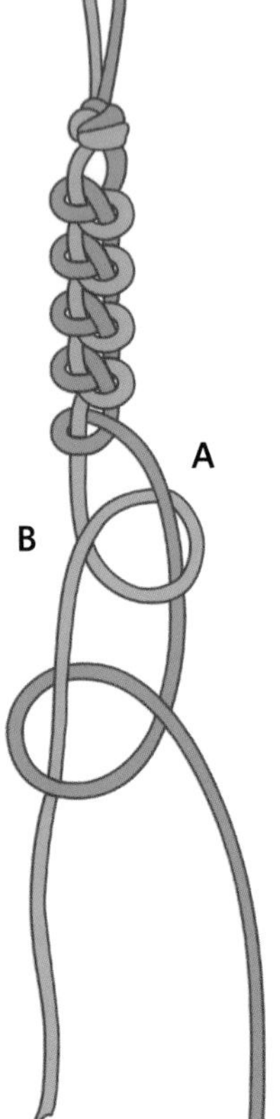

ALTERNATING HALF-HITCH KNOT

The secret to tying this knot is to keep the tension on the correct thread as you work because each thread alternates between being used as the core thread and the knotting thread. You'll start by holding one thread taut as you loop the other around it and then you'll switch them so the core thread becomes the knotting thread and vice versa.

Note that the illustration includes two loose loops to show the relationship between the two threads as they're tied, but in reality, the first loop (shown in green) would have to be tightened before the other thread (in blue) can be looped and tied.

Step 1: Tie two threads together on one end using an overhand knot. Hold one of the threads straight and taut to serve as the core (A, shown in blue) and then bring the knotting thread (B, in green) from the left and loop it over and around the core, exiting to the left and pulling it tightly around the core.

Step 2: To make the next loop, the knotting thread becomes the core thread (shown in green). Hold the green thread taut and loop the blue thread from the right side over and around it, exiting to the right and pulling it tightly around the green core. Repeat, switching thread tensions and looping back and forth to create the alternating pattern, pulling tightly after tying each loop before starting the next.

LARK'S HEAD KNOT

A lark's head knot consists of two complete loops tied around a core thread: The first loop goes over the core and then the second loop goes under it. One thread serves as the core, while the other is used to tie all the knots. This knot can also be worked either from right to left (as shown in the main illustration on the right) or from left to right (shown on the far right).

Step 1: Tie the two threads together at one end using an overhand knot. Hold the core thread (shown in blue) straight and taut. Bring the knotting thread (in green) to the right side of the core thread and then loop it *over* and around the core, exiting to the right as shown (A).

Step 2: Pull the loop tight around the core and then pass the knotting thread *under* and around the core thread, exiting through to the right as shown (B). Pull the second loop tight to complete the knot.

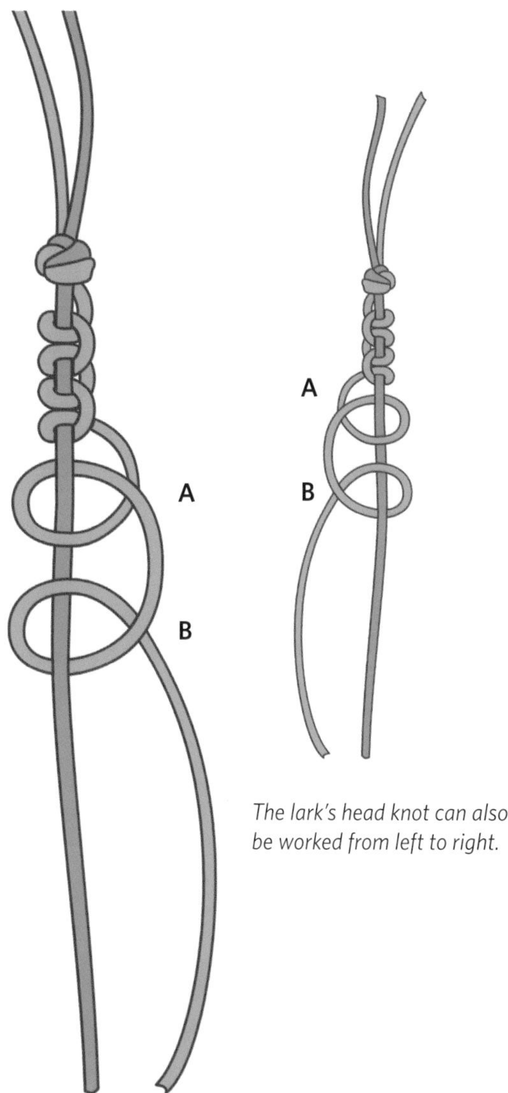

The lark's head knot can also be worked from left to right.

ALTERNATING LARK'S HEAD KNOT

Step 1: Tie three cords together on one end using an overhand knot. Pull one straight down to serve as the core.

Step 2: Tie a lark's head knot with the left cord and then with the cord on the right. Alternate by working side to side over the core. If you are working with two colors, this produces a design that forms one solid color down each side.

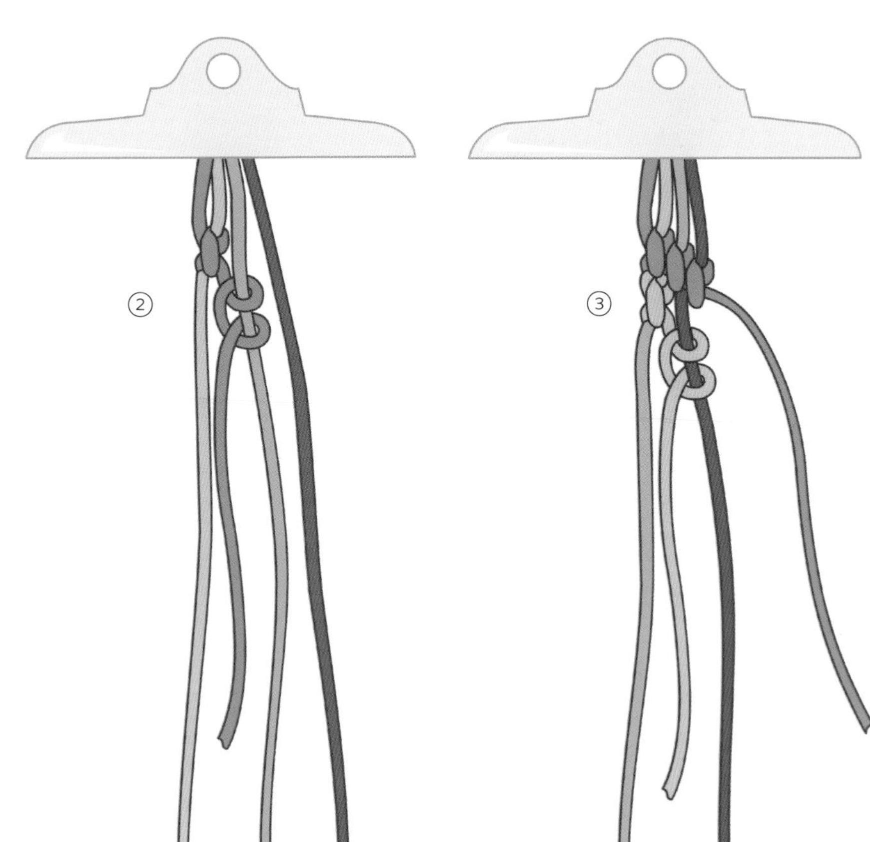

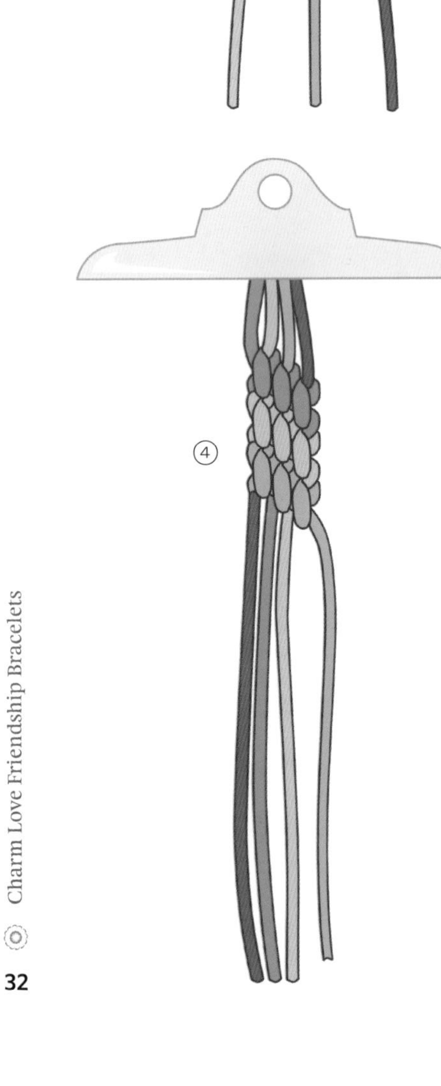

DIAGONAL STRIPES

Step 1: Tie four threads together and arrange them from left to right. Take the thread from the left (blue) and tie a double half-hitch around the next thread in the line (yellow). Pull tight after each loop to complete one knot.

Step 2: Move to the next thread to the right (green) and tie the same blue thread over the green thread with a double half-hitch knot. Continue to the last thread (purple) and tie a double half-hitch knot over this with the blue thread. The blue thread will now be in the last position in the row.

Step 3: Begin the new row with the first thread (yellow) on the left and tie it over each thread along the row with a double half-hitch knot over each thread as you did in the previous steps.

Step 4: After completing each row, start with the new thread on the left, moving to the right. A downward diagonal striped pattern will form as you progress.

CHEVRON

Step 1: Start by folding three long threads in half to give you six and then knot them at the folded end to secure. Bring all six threads down and separate them. Arrange them across with the blue threads on the far left and far right and the green threads next to each other in the middle. For this step, you will be tying the first thread (blue) on the left around the next two core threads along a row using a double half-hitch knot. Tie a double half-hitch knot over the second thread (yellow), keeping the yellow thread nice and taut. Now move to the next thread (green) and tie a half-hitch knot over it. The blue thread is now in the center.

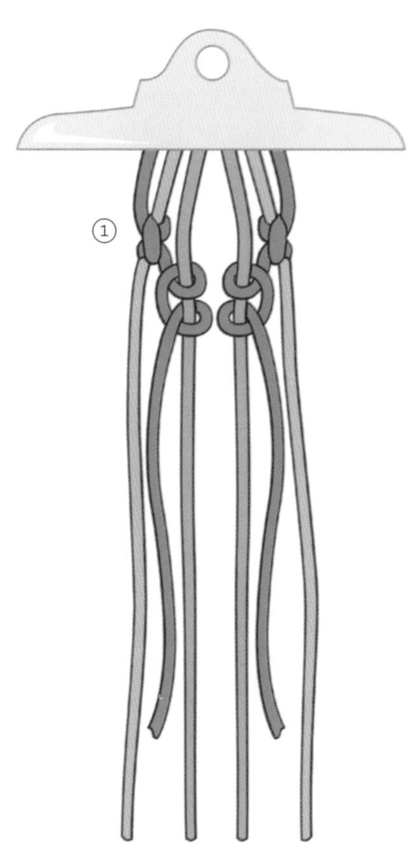

Step 2: In step 1, you tied knots from left to right moving towards the center. In this step, start on the right and move left toward the center. Pick up the blue thread on the right and tie a double half-hitch knot over the yellow thread and then the green threads, moving towards the center. Finish by taking one of the blue threads and tying a double half-hitch over the other to form a knot in the center. It doesn't matter whether you start with the left or right blue thread to form the center knot. This completes one row of the chevron pattern.

Step 3: Repeat step 2, but begin with the yellow threads on the far left and right. Tie over each thread moving towards the center. Tie one yellow thread over the other in the center with a double half-hitch knot to complete row two.

Step 4: Keep forming rows by starting with the outside threads and moving toward the center. To avoid creating holes, be sure to tie a knot in the center with the matching colors to complete each row.

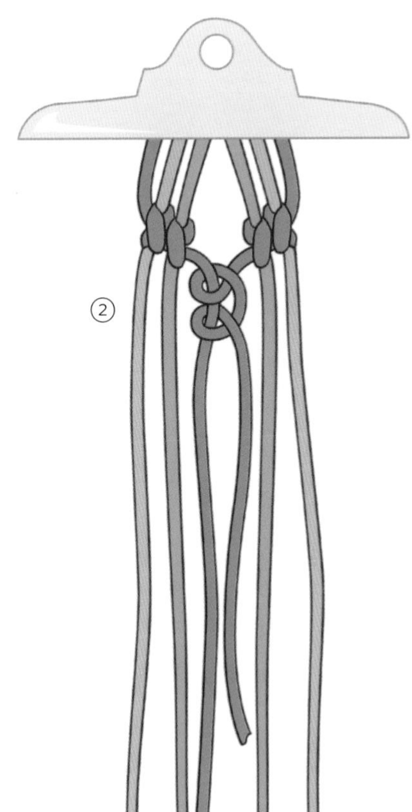

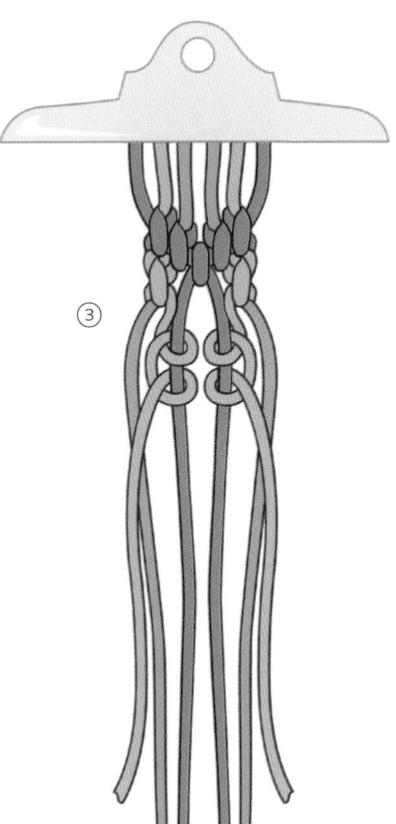

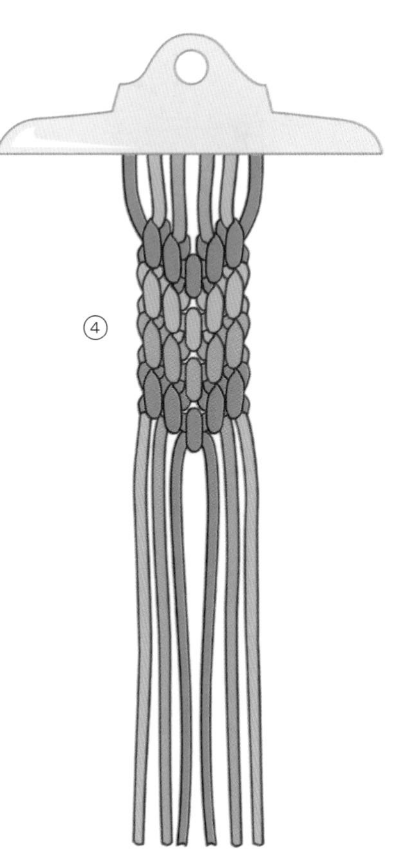

DIAMOND/CHEVRON COMBINATION

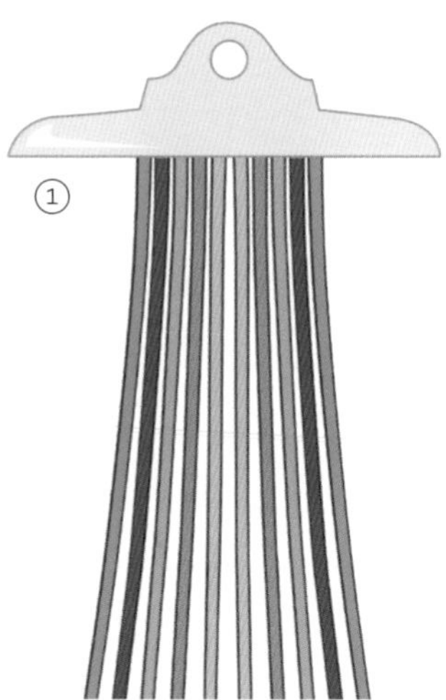

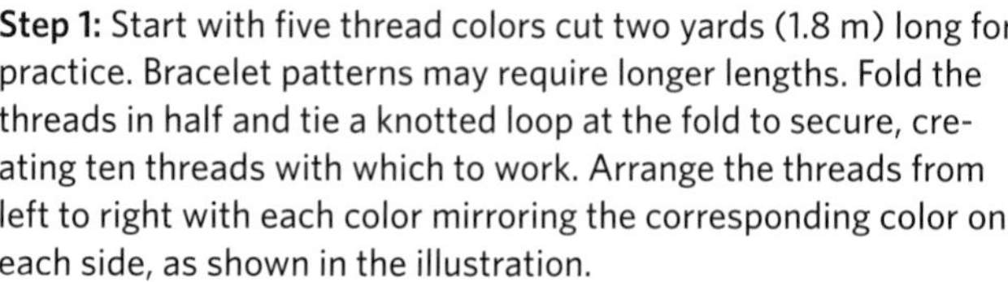

Step 1: Start with five thread colors cut two yards (1.8 m) long for practice. Bracelet patterns may require longer lengths. Fold the threads in half and tie a knotted loop at the fold to secure, creating ten threads with which to work. Arrange the threads from left to right with each color mirroring the corresponding color on each side, as shown in the illustration.

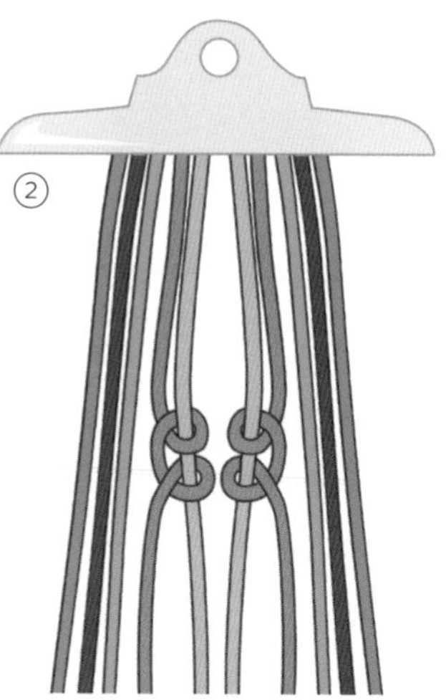

Step 2: With steps 2 and 3, you are creating a triangle of knots to fill in space before beginning the chevron pattern. Start with the tan thread to the left of the left center yellow thread and tie a double half-hitch knot around the yellow thread with the tan thread (double half-hitch to the right). Repeat the same knot using the tan thread from the right side. Tie a double half-hitch with the right tan thread around the yellow thread to the left of it (double half-hitch to the left).

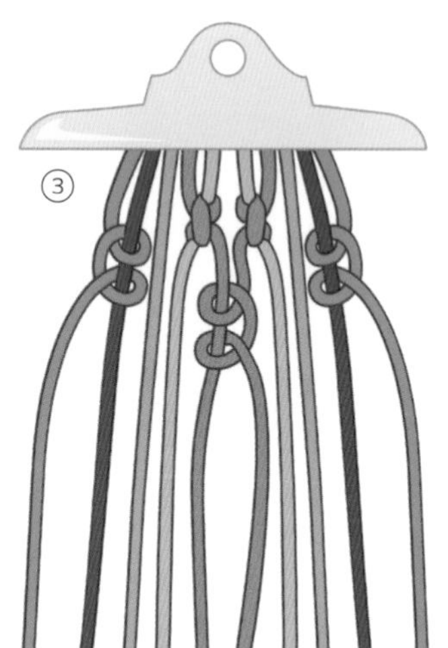

Step 3: Tie a double half-hitch knot with the tan threads in the center. It doesn't matter which thread you use to start. Now you can begin the chevron pattern. This illustration shows where to begin with the blue threads at each end (far left and far right). Half-hitch knots are tied around each sequential thread moving towards the middle from each side.

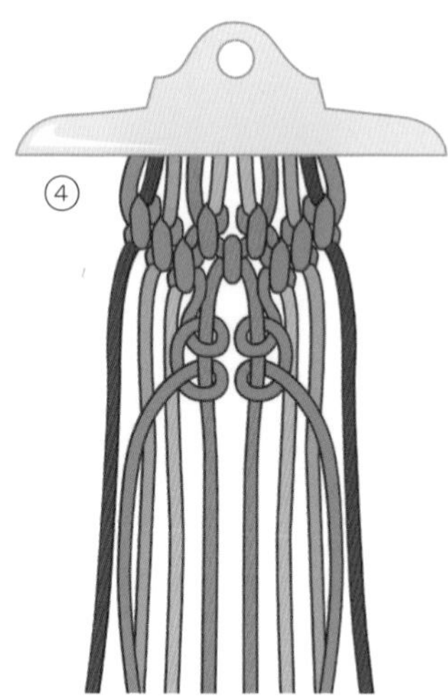

Step 4: Tie half-hitch knots over each thread from both sides until both blue threads meet in the middle (four double half-hitch knots to the right and four double half-hitch knots to the left).

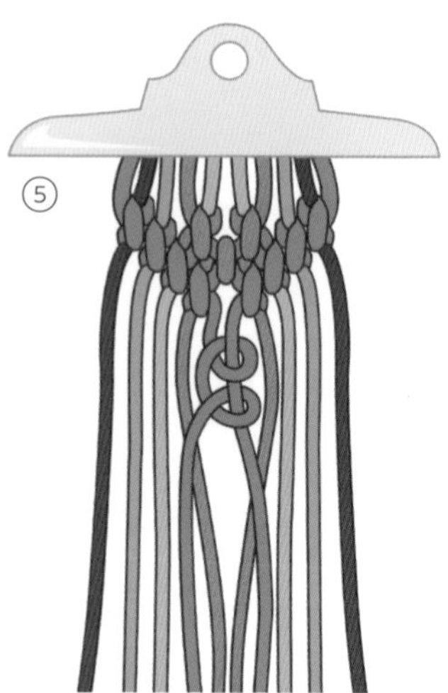

Step 5: Tie a double half-hitch knot in the center with the blue threads. Again, it won't matter which side is used first.

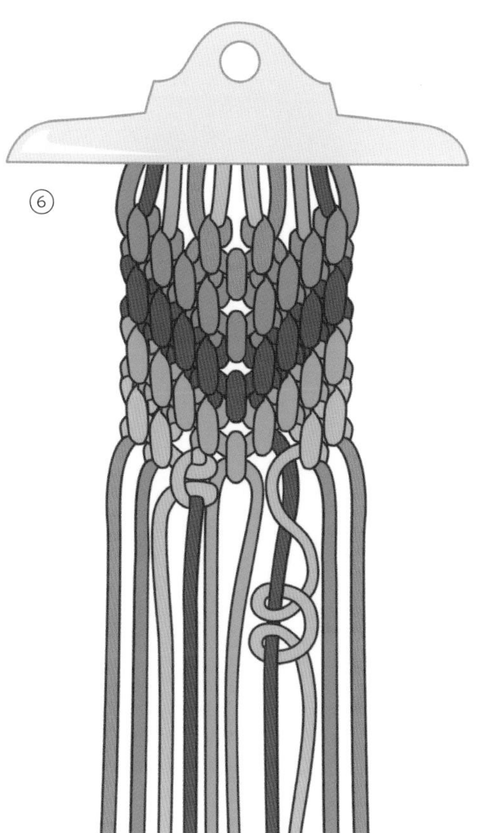

Step 6: Continue following steps 4 and 5 to create chevron stripes for the desired number of rows. Always start with the outside threads of the same color, working towards the center. End in the middle with a double half-hitch knot. To begin a diamond pattern, you will need to reverse the direction of some threads by tying a lark's head knot instead of a double half-hitch. The yellow threads in this illustration are tied over the tan and blue threads with double half-hitch knots working towards the center. When you reach the purple thread, tie a lark's head knot instead. To tie this knot, form the first loop in the same way you have been tying the previous knots. However, as you begin to tie the second loop of the knot, pass the yellow thread under the purple thread to make the loop, which will result in a lark's head. The yellow knot on the left shows a completed lark's head knot, while the one on the right shows the knot in progress. Notice the placement of the yellow threads after the knot is tied. Do not tie anything around the green threads from the previous row.

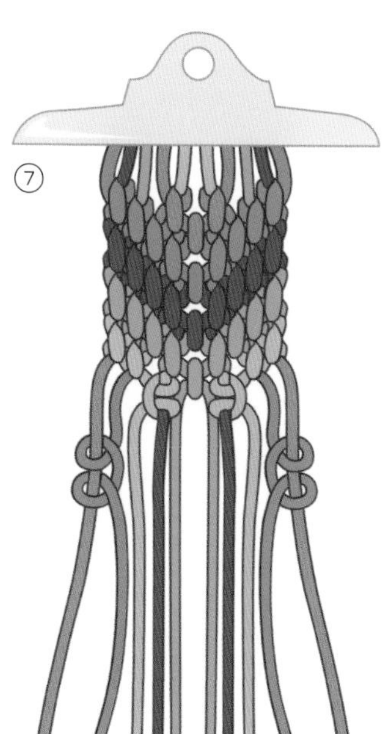

Step 7: Tie the second blue thread over the first left tan thread with a double half-hitch to the left. Repeat on the right side, tying to the right.

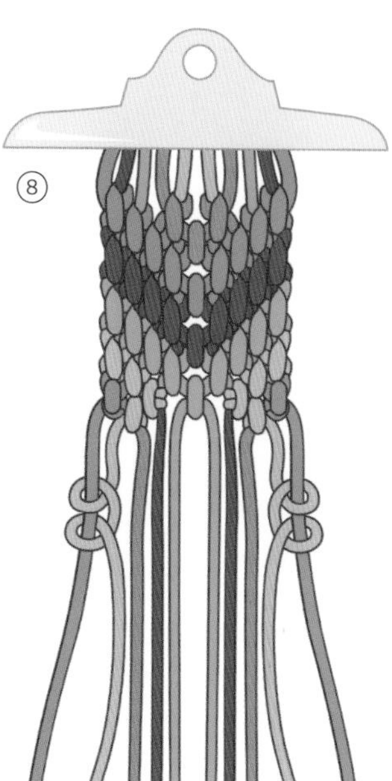

Step 8: Tie diagonal half-hitch knots with the yellow thread over each thread, working out to the left. Repeat with the thread on the right, working over each thread to the right.

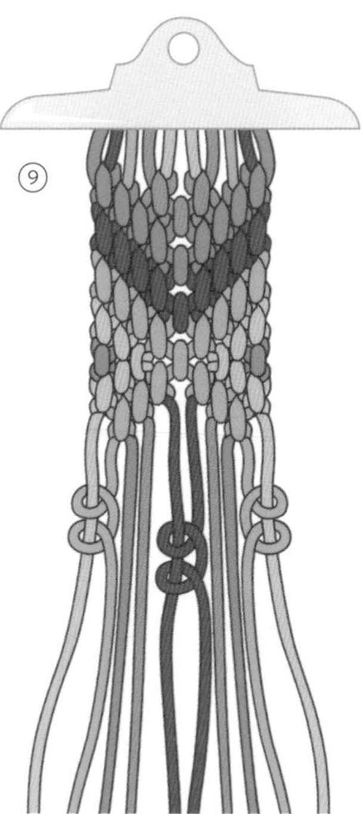

Step 9: For this row, start in the center with the green threads and tie double half-hitch knots out to each side over each thread. Now the purple threads will be in the center. Tie the purple threads together with a half-hitch knot to begin the new row.

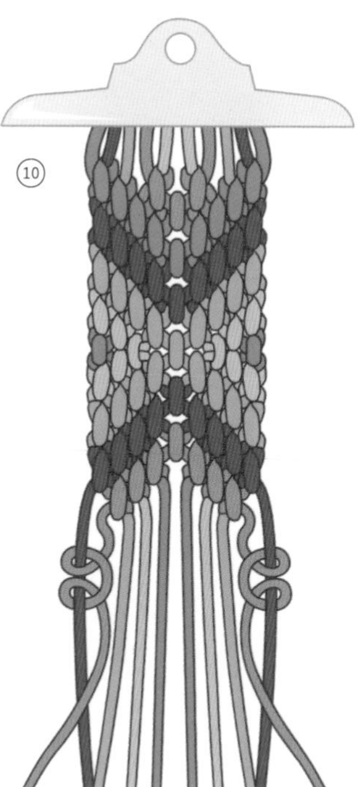

Step 10: Repeat step 9 with each color, starting from the center and working out for the desired number of chevron rows. When you are ready to start a center diamond pattern, tie a lark's head knot over the last thread on each side, as shown with the tan thread over the purple thread in this illustration.

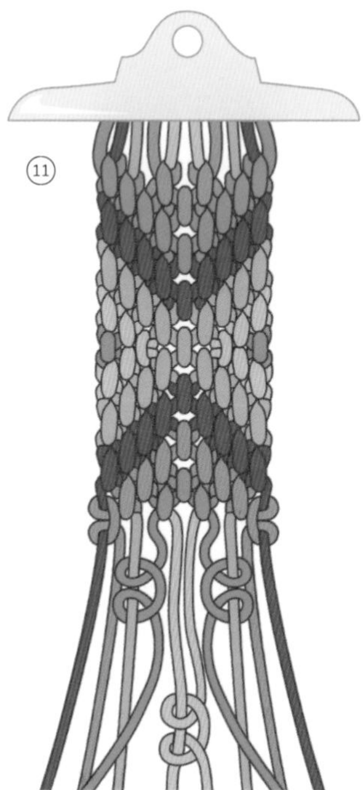

Step 11: For the next row, tie the blue threads, starting from the center and working out. Stop at the green threads and tie a lark's head knot on each side over the green threads as shown. Tie the yellow threads in the center with one double half-hitch knot.

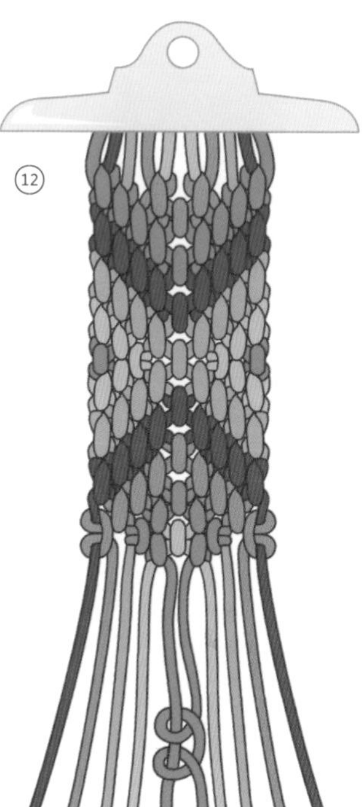

Step 12: Tie the blue threads back towards the middle with double half-hitch knots, tying them together in the center.

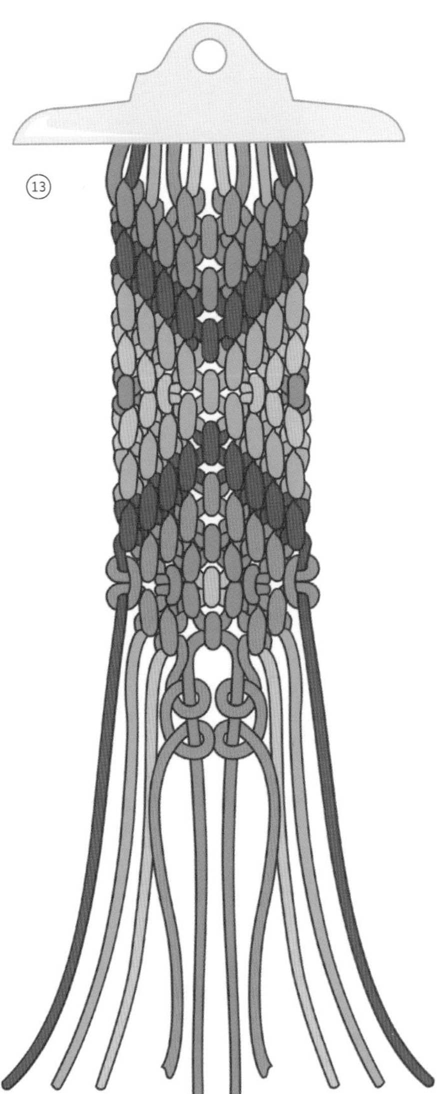

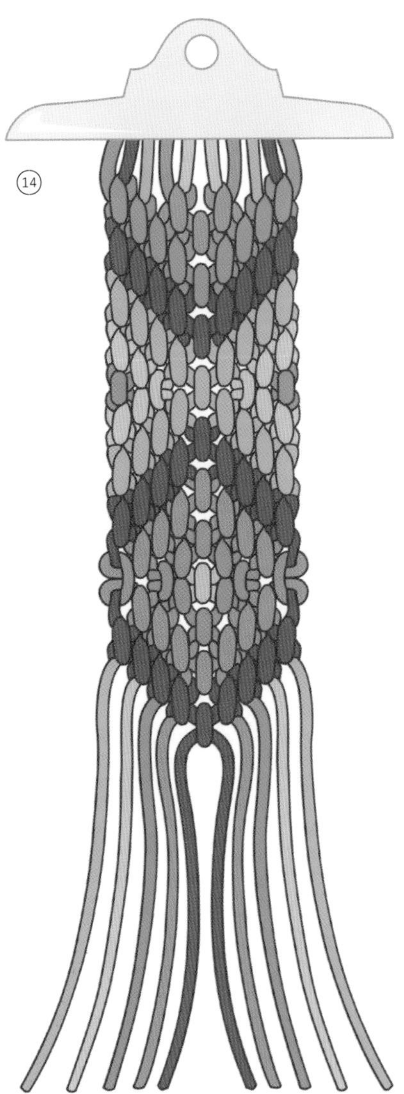

Step 13: Tie the tan threads over each thread, working toward the middle with double half-hitch knots. Tie the tan threads together in the center.

Step 14: Now you are back to the beginning of the pattern (see step 4 to start over). Tie the far purple threads toward the center to create the next row. Jump in at step 6 when you are satisfied with the number of rows desired.

Starting and Finishing a Bracelet

There are several ways to start and finish a bracelet. For the simplest approach, tie loose ends around your wrist or make a fancy knotted loop and button closure. Here is a handy guide for bracelet ends you can mix and match.

STARTING A BRACELET

Simple Knot
The easiest way to start a bracelet is to tie a simple overhand knot as shown in the illustration on page 25. Leave a length of cord(s) free above the knot, which will be needed to tie the bracelet.

Simple Loop

This knot looks best when used with just one cord, such as a piece of thin leather or waxed linen. Double the cord to create a loop and then tie an overhand knot at the base to secure. Use this loop for a button closure or to fasten loose cord ends.

Braided Loop

Braid three or more threads at the center of your work consisting of long lengths of cut threads. Braid them for a short length and then form a loop with the braided section by bringing the threads together. Tie a knot to secure the ends.

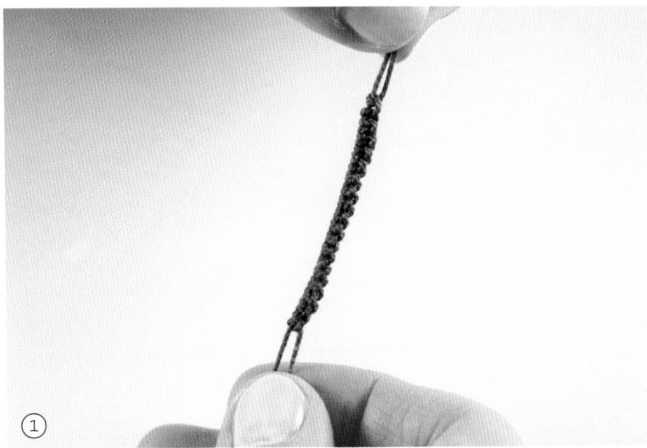

Lark's Head Loop

This loop has an extra fancy look that works well for a button closure or to fasten cord ends. For this knot, you'll need two threads, one about 12 inches (30.5 cm) longer than the other.

Step 1: Gather the ends of both threads and then find the mid-point of the shorter thread. At that point, use the longer thread to tie a series of lark's head knots over the shorter thread. Tie a series of knots until the section is long enough to form a loop. The longer thread will become shorter than the core thread.

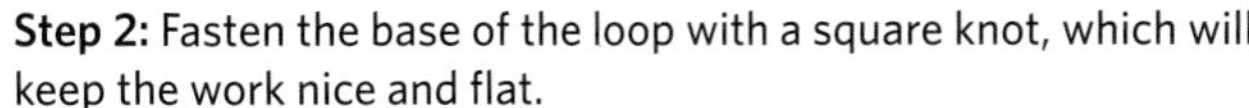

Step 2: Fasten the base of the loop with a square knot, which will keep the work nice and flat.

Loose Threads with Bead Ends
A bracelet can be finished with loose threads in the same way one can be started. Simply tie the threads together to fasten around the wrist. The ends can be embellished with beads using overhand knots to secure them. If you use beads with large holes, several threads will fit through a single bead as a possible design option.

Braided Ends
Instead of simply leaving loose threads to finish the end of a bracelet, consider braiding the threads. If you have six or more loose threads, divide them into two groups and braid each group to create two braided strands to be used as ties. Finish the braided ends with overhand knots. Tie the braided strands through a loop at the other end of the bracelet to fasten.

Button End
A button made of clay makes a decorative closure to use with a loop. Either bring the thread ends together through the holes on the button or through a wire shank on the back of the button and tie a knot under the button to secure. Plan ahead to ensure the button will fit through the loop you design.

Adjustable Square Knot Slide

Bring the loose thread ends towards each other and then overlap them. Use a 12 inch (30.5 cm) scrap piece of thread to tie a square knot slide over the ends. Tie a few square knots in a row over the core threads. Trim off the ends of the square knot threads and core threads and glue or seal with heat, depending on the stringing material being used.

Jewelry Making Tools and Findings

The bracelet designs in this book are created by using simple knotting techniques (see pages 25–37 for details), so you'll need just a few jewelry making tools and findings to refine and complete your projects.

DESIGN ELEMENTS

Findings—elements such as clasps, jump rings, metal bezels, and pieces of filigree—are used in a variety of ways to connect the components of a design and to give it a finished, professional look. For example, jump rings can be used to connect charms to bracelet threads, while metal findings like filigree can be incorporated into a charm design by baking them right into polymer clay.

Metal and glass beads can be used to complement polymer clay charms by creating repetition or balance within a bracelet's knotted design.

Chain or rhinestone strands can be woven or sewn into a bracelet's knotwork to add sparkle and enhance its structure.

BASIC TOOLS

To form and cut wire, attach jump rings, and add findings, you'll need **wire cutters** and two types of pliers—**round nose pliers** for creating loops and wrapping wire and **chain nose pliers** for shaping and bending wire. **Jewelry tweezers** are great for placing tiny beads on clay or for pulling delicate threads.

GLUES AND SEALERS FOR THREADS

Two-part epoxy can be used to attach elements and embellishments; to secure beads, clay, or stones to or around bezels; and to seal the ends of cords and threads. Use the clear, fast-setting two-part epoxies that are commonly found in hardware stores. **White glue** and **fabric sealant** may also be used to seal thread ends, especially if you prefer to use a nontoxic glue that cleans up with soap and water.

Another option for finishing and sealing threads is a **thread melting tool,** which melts and seals the cut ends of nylon cord to keep it from raveling. Thread melting tools can be found at bead stores and through beading supply companies.

Jewelry-Making Techniques

Here are a few basic jewelry techniques you will need to know for some of the projects that involve attaching clay charms, accent beads, and jewelry findings such as clasps.

OPENING AND CLOSING A JUMP RING

To open a jump ring, you will need two pairs of chain nose pliers.

Step 1: With the seam of the jump ring at the top, hold the ring on both sides with the pliers. Do not pull the jump ring open and apart as this weakens the jump ring, adding stress to the metal. Instead, pull one of the pliers towards you and push the other pair away from you to open the jump ring.

Step 2: To close the jump ring, bring the wires back to meet in the center from the sides in the same fashion as they were opened.

MAKING A WRAPPED WIRE LOOP

In some of the designs in this book, I've added small accent beads to complement the polymer clay beads. To add beads, thread a bead onto a head pin wire, forming a loop at the top of the wire to attach the bead to a bracelet.

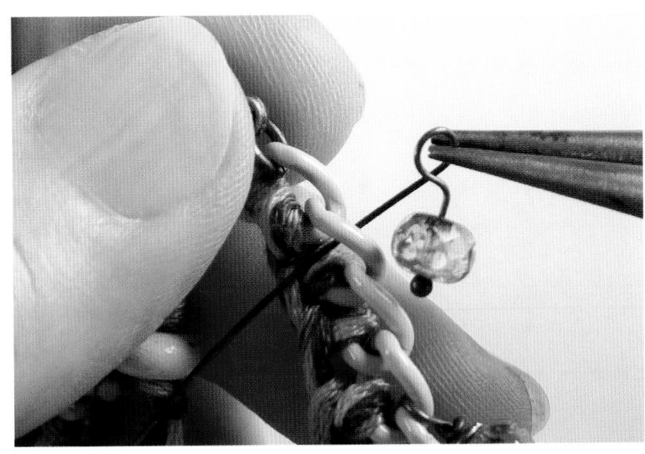

Add a bead to the head pin and form a 90-degree bend in the wire. Using the round nose pliers, bend the wire into a loop. Attach the loop to the bracelet and then hold the loop with pliers. Wrap the wire around the base of the loop a few times to secure. Trim the excess wire with wire cutters and tuck in the end of the wire with chain nose pliers.

CHAPTER THREE

CHARM LOVE DESIGNS

Lucky Charms

Small vintage charms were used to mold polymer clay replicas for this project. In addition to featuring the imagery of the vintage charms, translucent clay is used to replicate pressed or cast glass in the Czech tradition. Pressed or cast glass beads have a long history, originating with beads produced in the Czech Republic that date back to the fourteenth century. Translucent clay creates a glasslike effect that mimics the look and feel of cast glass.

FOR THE CHARMS

- Miniature gumball machine charms or figures
- Two-part silicone mold putty
- Rubber gloves
- Translucent polymer clay (such as Pardo)
- Alcohol inks in red, blue, green, and cream
- Craft knife
- Needle tool or clay sculpting tool
- Wire loop or eye pin finding
- Baking tray and sheet of paper or silicone mat
- Gilders paste wax
- Two-part epoxy resin, toothpick, waxed paper, and small rhinestones (optional)

①

②

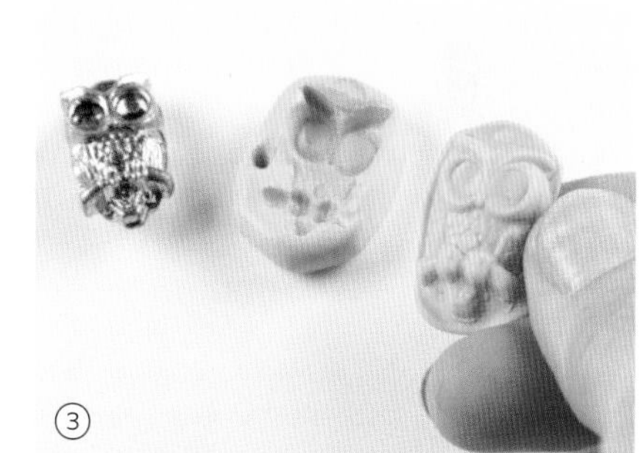
③

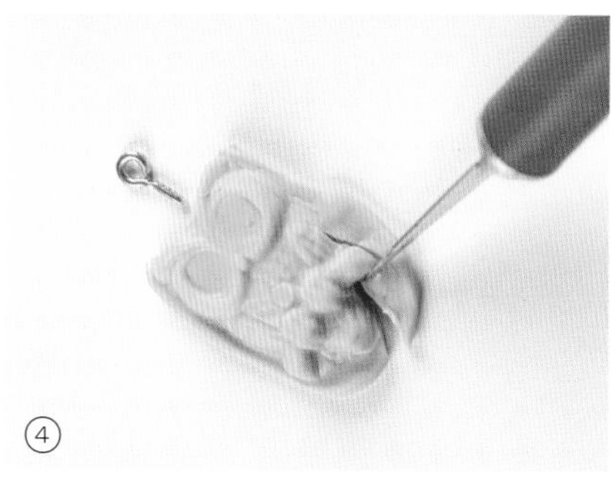
④

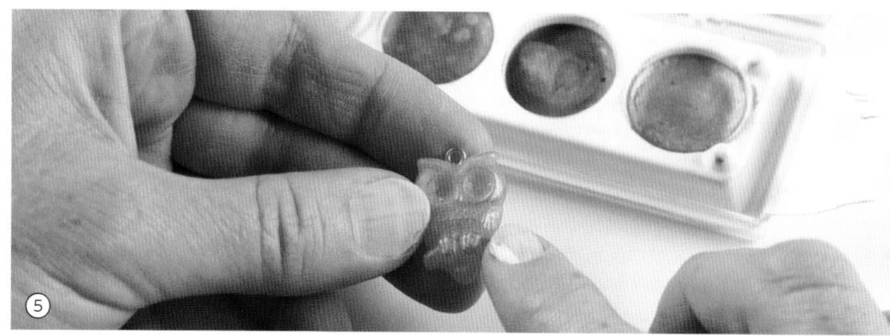
⑤

Step 1: Make silicone putty molds by pressing small objects or charms into the putty (see page 19). Use the finished molds to cast the charms.

Step 2: Tint a small ball of clay by kneading in a few drops of alcohol ink until the color is even. The clay will be very pale and opaque in color, but it will intensify after baking. (Tip: Wearing rubber gloves will keep you from staining your fingers.)

Step 3: Press the tinted clay into the mold and then remove. This photo shows the original piece, the mold, and the cast clay charm.

Step 4: Use a craft knife to trim the excess clay from the edges of the cast charm. Refine or add details if desired using a needle or clay shaper tool. Insert a wire loop or eye pin into the top of the clay charm prior to baking. Bake the clay charms on a baking tray as directed by the manufacturer. Remove from the oven and let cool.

Step 5: Highlight the texture of the charm with gilders paste wax to complement the color and sheen of the charm. To add rhinestones for the owl charm's eyes (as shown in the finished bracelet on page 46), mix a small amount of epoxy resin to affix the eyes to the clay.

FOR THE BRACELET

2 yards (1.8 m) green nylon bead cord

2 yards (1.8 m) yellow nylon bead cord

Small jump rings

Lobster claw clasp

Chain nose pliers

Thread melting tool

Step 1: Double the cords and tie a series of lark's head knots with one of the cords tied over the other. Tie enough knots to make a small loop as shown on page 39. Tie a square knot under the loop and then begin the knotting pattern. Pull one green thread and one yellow thread to the center to serve as the core.

Step 2: An alternating lark's head knot, shown on page 31, is used to form the pattern. One side will be tied with the yellow thread and the other side with green. Tie a lark's head knot on one side with one cord tied over the core cords and then switch and tie a lark's head knot on the other side with the opposite cord. One color will form to the right and one to the left for the length of the bracelet. To finish the bracelet, tie a lobster claw clasp with a jump ring attaching it to the end of the cord. Seal the knot by burning the ends with a thread burner tool. Use pliers to attach the clay charms to the bracelet with jump rings.

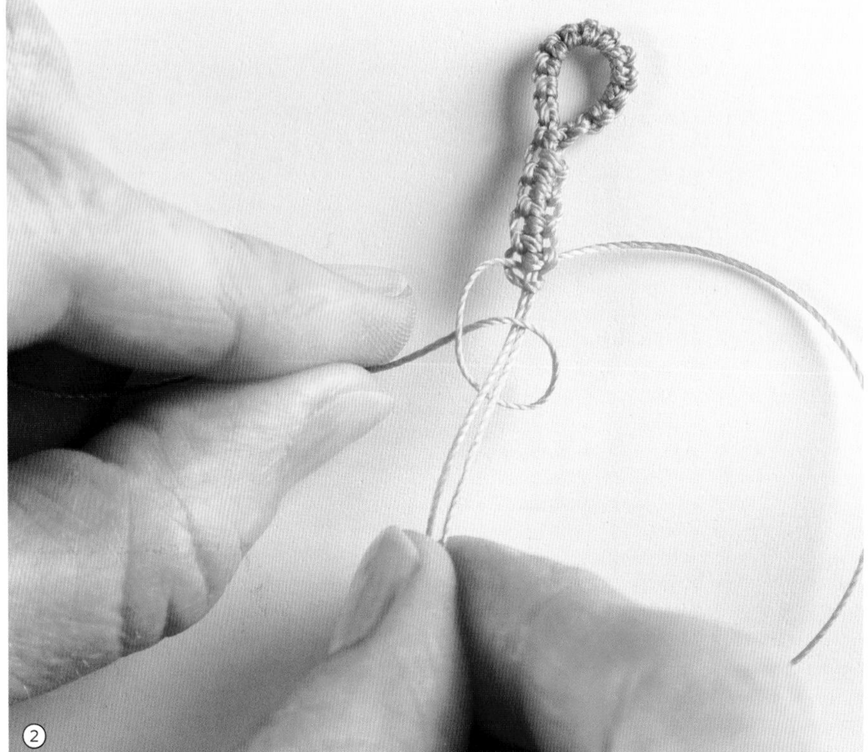

VARIATION

Rolling in the Deep

Collect starfish, seashells, and sea urchins and use them to make silicone molds. The molds pick up every detail of the intricate textures found on seashells. Tinted translucent polymer clay is pressed into the molds to make ocean inspired charms that give off a translucent glow, like glass from the sea.

FOR THE CHARMS

- Small seashells in various shapes
- Two-part silicone mold putty
- Rubber gloves
- Translucent polymer clay (such as Pardo)
- Alcohol inks
- Craft knife
- Needle tool
- Wire loop or eye pin finding
- Gilders paste wax

FOR THE BRACELET

- 2 yards (1.8 m) aqua nylon bead cord
- 2 yards (1.8 m) light green nylon bead cord
- Jump rings
- Lobster claw clasp
- Head pins
- Glass beads
- Pliers
- Wirecutters

MAKING THE CHARMS

①

②

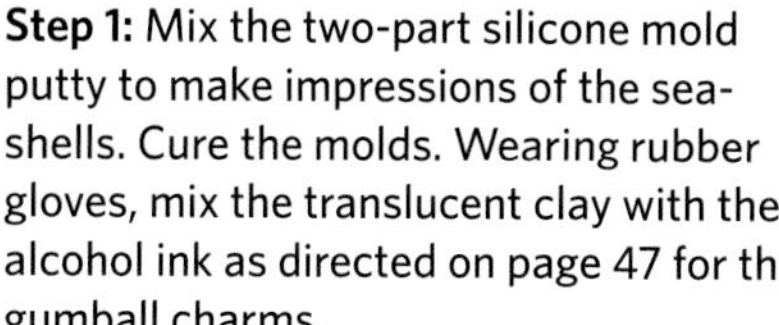

Step 1: Mix the two-part silicone mold putty to make impressions of the seashells. Cure the molds. Wearing rubber gloves, mix the translucent clay with the alcohol ink as directed on page 47 for the gumball charms.

Step 2: Press tinted clay into the prepared molds. Trim the edges of the clay with a craft knife and refine the charm edges with clay shaper tool. Insert a wire loop or eye pin into the top of the charm and bake.

KNOTTING THE BRACELET

To knot the bracelet, follow the instructions on page 48 for Lucky Charms, using the aqua and light green cords. Tie a lobster claw clasp to the end of the bracelet. Follow the instructions on page 43 to attach the charms with jump rings. Thread extra beads onto the head pins as shown on page 43.

Dead Heads

Sugar skulls, commonly used to decorate Day of the Dead festivities, were the inspiration for this bold black-and-white design. Skulls are easy to sculpt. Start with a light bulb shape and then add details with a needle tool. Embellish the skulls with rhinestones, colorful clay flowers, and paint.

FOR THE BEADS

- White polymer clay
- Bits of pink and green polymer clay
- Round wooden toothpicks
- Small faceted rhinestones
- Black acrylic paint
- Brown antiquing medium
- Needle tool
- Craft knife
- Paper towel

①

HINT *You can pierce the skull bead with a toothpick and leave it in place to maintain the bead hole while sculpting the details and adding rhinestones and other embellishments. Twist the toothpick gently to remove before baking.*

②

③

Step 1: Sculpt a skull shape using a small ball of white polymer clay. Pinch the jaw area to narrow it, leaving the head round. Use the pink clay to form five small petals for a flower to place on the skull and the green clay to create a small ball for the flower's center. Make accent beads as desired, such as heart shaped bones. Optional: Make four small beads with large holes to use as bracelet ends.

Step 2: Use a rounded clay tool to form eye sockets on the skull. Pierce a hole in the center of each socket with a needle tool to mark placement for a faceted rhinestone for each eye. Push the pointed back rhinestones into the sockets. Use a craft knife or needle tool to add finishing details such as nostrils, teeth, and eyelashes. Add the flower petals to the head and anchor them in place using the end of a needle tool. Press the small green ball of the clay into the center of the petals. Use a needle tool to pierce a hole through the skull from side to side for stringing. Bake the clay beads.

Step 3: Mix black acrylic paint with brown antiquing medium to stain the recessed details of the beads. The gel helps to keep the paint moving into the crevices while rubbing off of the surface. The brown color of the gel imparts an antique look to the white color of the clay. Rub the paint/gel into the crevices. Wipe the surface of the baked skull with a damp paper towel to remove the excess paint.

FOR THE BRACELET

4 yards (3.7 m) black nylon cord (cut into 2 pieces, 2 yards [1.8 m] each)

Fine wire for stringing

Black faceted beads with large holes

Scissors

Small clay beads

Thread burner tool

8 inch (20.5 cm) piece black curb chain

Two pairs of pliers for attaching chain

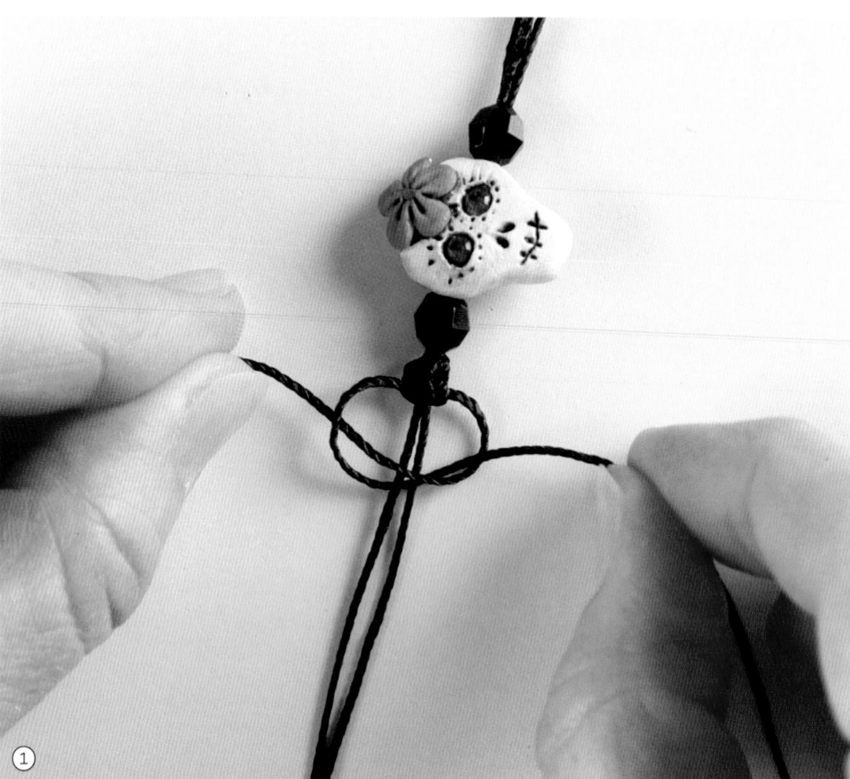
①

Step 1: Double both threads and attach a fine wire through both loops to thread through the beads. This will give you four strands to pass through. Thread faceted beads, skulls, and the heart bead, alternating each clay piece with a faceted bead. Slide the beads to the center of the cords. After all of the beads are strung, cut the loop ends. Starting on one side, pull the two cords to the center to serve as a core. Use the other two cords to tie square knots. Tie a series of square knots on each side of the beads to form the sides of the bracelet. Continue knotting until the desired length is achieved.

②

Step 2: Secure the end of the square knot pattern with an overhand knot on each side. Tie a sliding square knot closure over the ends of all the cords as shown on page 41. Add small clay beads to the ends of the cords to finish, securing with overhand knots. Use a thread burner tool to seal the ends of the cord after cutting. Measure a piece of black curb chain to match the length of the bracelet. Use pliers to open the end links of the chain and attach it close to the overhand knots at each end of the bracelet.

Pearl Glam

This bracelet features simple disk-shaped charms swirled with subtle color that appear dipped in silver for a young, fashion-forward look. Silver leaf, including composite types, can be found in craft stores; it is less expensive than real silver. Choose thread colors to match the polymer clay colors you are using. This bracelet features soft pastel shades of violet and white clay with a little bronze mixed in for warmth; this creates a pearlescent effect when combined with the silver leaf.

FOR THE CHARMS

- White polymer clay
- Small amounts of metallic clay in violet or other colors to create marbled texture
- Clay roller
- Round clay cutter
- Baking sheet
- Needle tool
- Three paintbrushes
- Gold leaf sizing
- Silver leaf
- Polymer clay varnish

Step 1: Start with a large conditioned ball of white polymer clay. Mix in very small amounts of metallic clay colors, violet, or other desired colors by twisting the colors into the white clay to marbleize. Use a clay roller to roll the clay into a flat sheet. Cut round disk shapes with a clay cutter. Shape one piece into a small oval to serve as a button closure. Use a needle tool to pierce holes at the top of each disk prior to baking. Pierce two holes in the oval-shaped button. Bake the disk shapes on a flat baking sheet.

Step 2: After the clay pieces are cool, embellish them with silver leaf. Use a paintbrush to apply liquid sizing, which will serve as an adhesive for the silver leaf. Cover half of the disk with the sizing. Let it dry until tacky.

Step 3: Apply the silver leaf using a soft brush to tap the leaf onto the disk. Don't worry if it looks a little messy; you can refine it after the sizing dries. If there are places on the surface where the leaf failed to stick, reapply the sizing and leaf to fill in the missing areas. Apply a bit of silver leaf to embellish the sides of the button. Seal the leaf and clay surface with polymer clay varnish.

FOR THE BRACELET

Embroidery floss (5 threads, cut to 3 yards [2.7 m] each in violet, pink, white, gray, and beige)

Fine wire for threading

Jump rings

Pliers

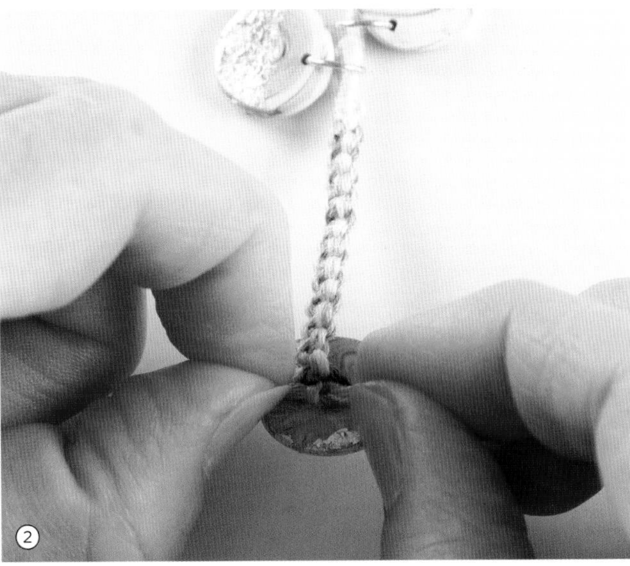

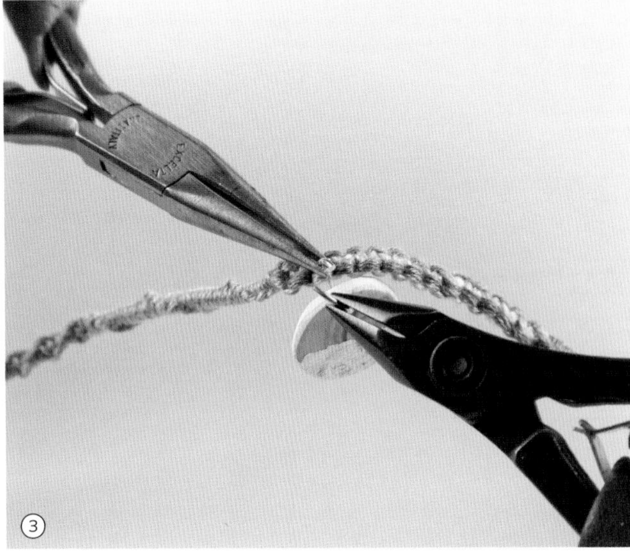

Step 1: Gather the threads and beginning about 6 inches (15 cm) down from the ends of the threads, use one of the threads to tie a series of lark's head knots over the other four, tying enough knots to form a loop that will fit over the button. Pull the 6 inch (15 cm) tail of threads down next to the long threads to form a larks head loop as shown on page 39. This will give you ten threads in all at the base of the loop. Tie a square knot to secure the threads. The five long threads will be used to knot the bracelet. Hide the short threads that remain from the 6 inch (15 cm) end into the work by tying a series of square knots over them with the longer threads. To tie the square knots, pull two long threads out to each side and tie them over the core, which consists of the short threads plus one long thread. Continue tying two types of knots, square knots and spiral half-hitch knots, to form the bracelet pattern. Tie each knot for about 1½ inches (4 cm) or as desired. Change the threads colors randomly along the way to add variety to the bracelet. This photo shows a square knot in progress. You can see previously tied spiral knots and so forth. Continue tying knots until you can wrap the bracelet twice around your wrist.

Step 2: Finish by passing the threads through the button and tying a knot to secure it on the back side.

Step 3: Use pliers to attach the disk charms along the bracelet threads with jump rings.

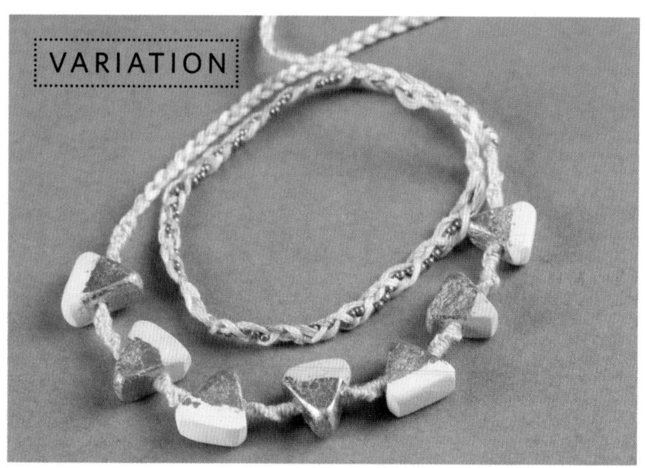

Golden Age

Try making geometric triangle shapes instead of traditional round beads to embellish a spiral wrap bracelet design. Imitation gold metal leaf was used to adorn the beads. A gold-toned ball chain was woven into the threads to complement the gold leaf, bringing it all together.

FOR THE CHARMS

- White polymer clay
- Orange polymer clay
- Three paintbrushes
- Gold leaf sizing
- Gold leaf (or composite faux gold leaf)
- Polymer clay varnish

FOR THE BRACELET

- Embroidery floss in three colors: 2 yards (1.8 m) orange thread, 1 yard (1 m) each of white and gray
- Fine ball chain

MAKING THE CHARMS

Step 1: Shape white and orange clay into small triangular bead shapes. Pierce and bake the beads. After the beads are cooled, embellish with gold leaf. Apply gold leaf and seal as directed for the silver leaf in the Pearl Glam project on page 54.

KNOTTING THE BRACELET

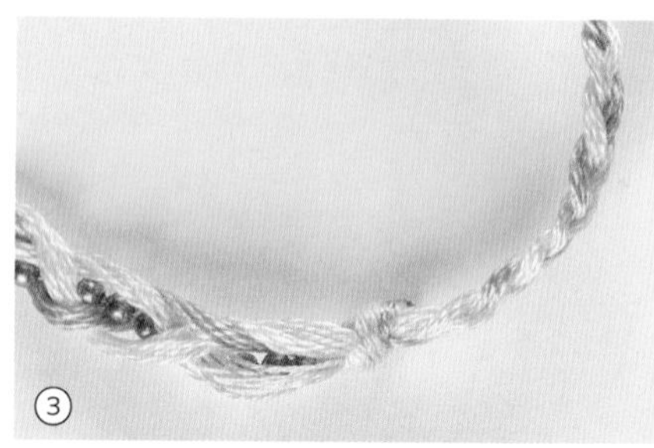

Step 1: Gather three threads (orange, gray, and white), leaving an 8 inch (20.5 cm) tail. Tie an overhand knot with all three threads. Tie a spiral half-hitch knot by tying the orange thread over the other two to form the bracelet pattern. Add triangle beads along the way, spacing them as desired. The spiral pattern is repeated between each bead (see photo above). After adding the beads, tie a few more spiral knots and then tie an overhand knot with all of the threads.

Step 2: The rest of the bracelet is formed using a braided pattern that incorporates chain. Braid a small ball chain in with one of the threads with a three-strand braid pattern. Continue until the bracelet is long enough to wrap around your wrist twice.

Step 3: Finish with an overhand knot. Braid the ends of the threads at both ends of the bracelet to serve as ties. Tie the bracelet around your wrist with the braided ends using a square knot.

Rainbow Ice

These beads look just like fired pottery. Start with a white clay base and then add dye-tinted liquid polymer to the surface. Let the colors bleed randomly for a "kiln-glazed" effect. Small eyelets provide neat looking ends for the beads to slide along the braided cord.

FOR THE BEADS

- White polymer clay
- Small metal eyelets
- Needle tool
- Metal leather stamping tools
- Liquid polymer clay
- Waxed paper
- Alcohol inks
- Toothpicks
- Paintbrush
- Tapered needle tool
- Embossing heat tool

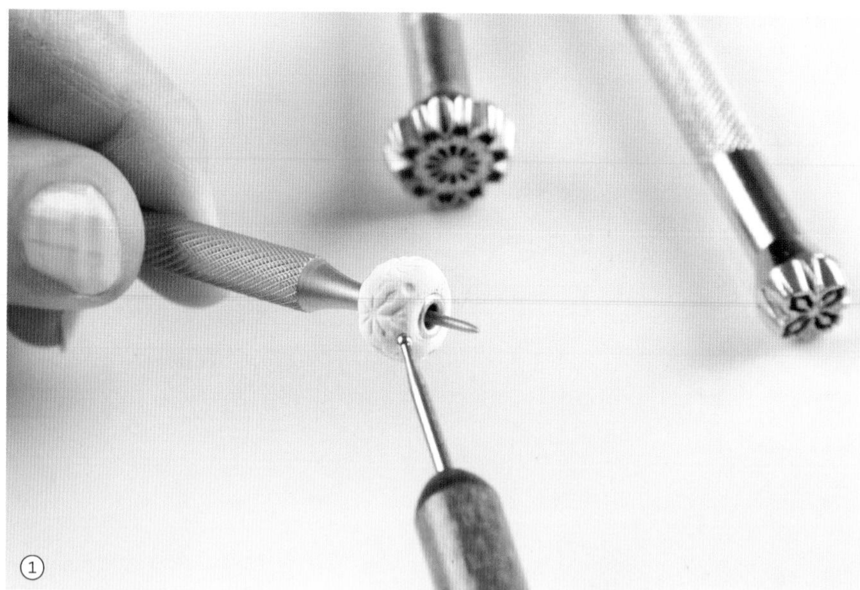

1

2

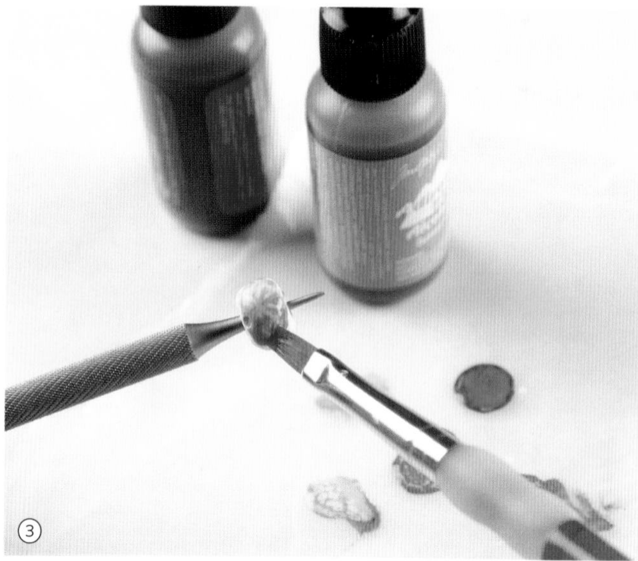

3

Step 1: To make a single bead, roll a small ball of clay to form a bead. Using the needle tool, pierce a hole through the clay that will be large enough for the eyelets to fit through. Press an eyelet into the holes on each side of the bead. Pass the needle tool through the bead to make sure the eyelets align. Make several beads for the bracelet. Stamp patterns around the beads using leather stamping tools or other textures. Bake the beads.

Step 2: Drop several pools of liquid polymer onto a sheet of waxed paper. Add a small drop of alcohol ink to each pool to create a palette of colors. Mix each color into the liquid clay with a toothpick.

Step 3: Make sure your heat tool is nearby and ready to use. Then, working with one bead at a time, use a metal tapered needle tool to hold the bead as you paint and heat the bead. Paint a layer of liquid polymer onto the surface of a cured bead, using various colors and letting them bleed into one another. Gently rotate the bead to keep the polymer from dripping off the bead.

Step 4: Cure the liquid polymer on the bead with an embossing heat tool. Twirl the needle tool as you heat to prevent the polymer from dripping off or burning. The polymer will start to become transparent and the colors more brilliant as you work. As soon as the polymer looks shiny and transparent, turn off the heat and cool the bead. The surface of the liquid polymer will harden as the bead cools.

KNOTTING THE BRACELET

FOR THE BRACELET

- Gray nylon bead cord, two pieces, cut 50 inches (127 cm) each
- Lobster claw clasp
- Fine wire for threading
- Scissors
- Glue or thread burner tool

Step 1: Double two 50 inch (127 cm) cords. Make a lark's head loop to start the bracelet by tying one cord over the other with a series of lark's head knots as shown on page 39.

Step 2: Form the length of the bracelet with a four-strand braid as shown on page 26. Thread beads onto the braided cord. After adding the beads, tie a loose overhand knot with all of the cords to secure the ends.

Step 3: Add a lobster claw clasp by threading the end of the cords through the clasp and back down through the loose overhand knot. Use a fine wire to aid the threading. Pull the knot tight and use scissors to clip off the excess cord. Finish the knot by sealing it with glue or use a thread burner tool.

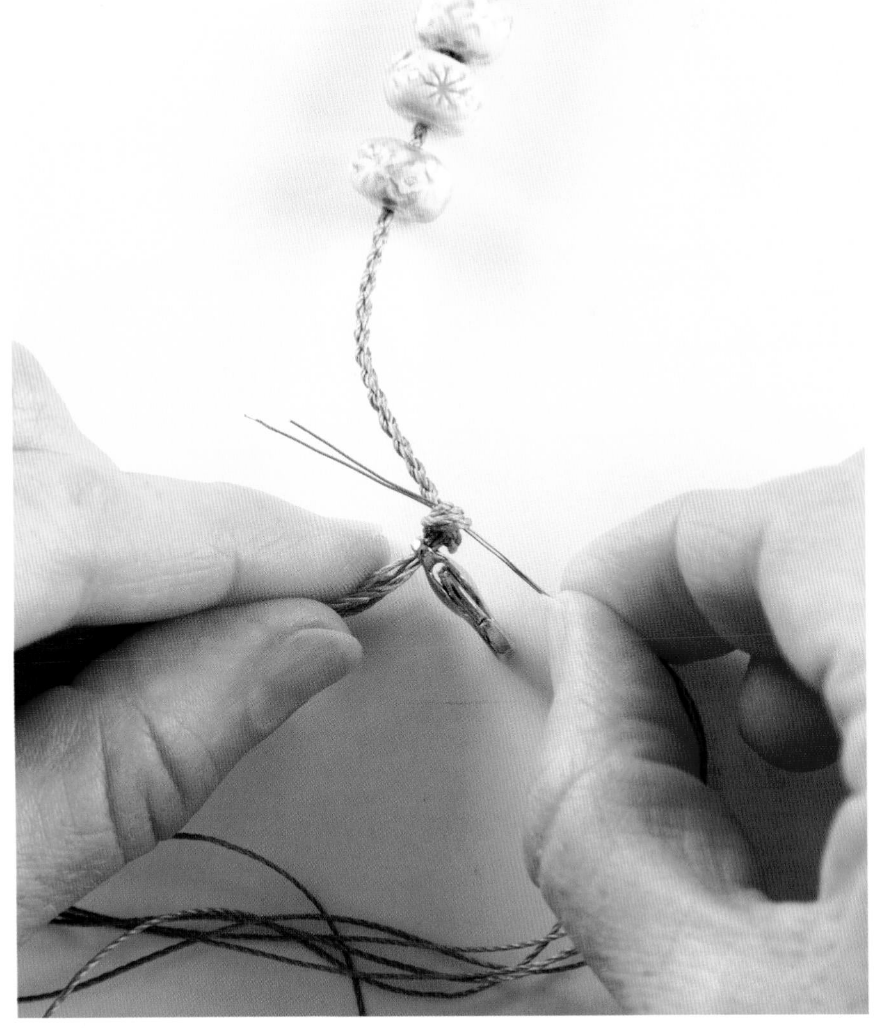

Branching Out

To make a delicate piece such as a branch in polymer clay, it is helpful to start with a wire armature to support and strengthen the clay. Wire loops on the ends of the branch are left exposed to allow cord to be attached to the branch. Embellish the branch with beads, clay flowers, and leaves. Celebrate the changing seasons by choosing different clay colors and beads to suit your mood.

FOR THE CHARM

- Bronze or brown, white, and pink polymer clay
- 8 inch (20.5 cm) piece of wire (metal or plastic coated)
- Gold or bronze acrylic paint
- Yellow acrylic paint
- Leaf shaped bead
- Head pin
- Round nose pliers
- Clay shaper tool
- Needle tool
- Wire cutters

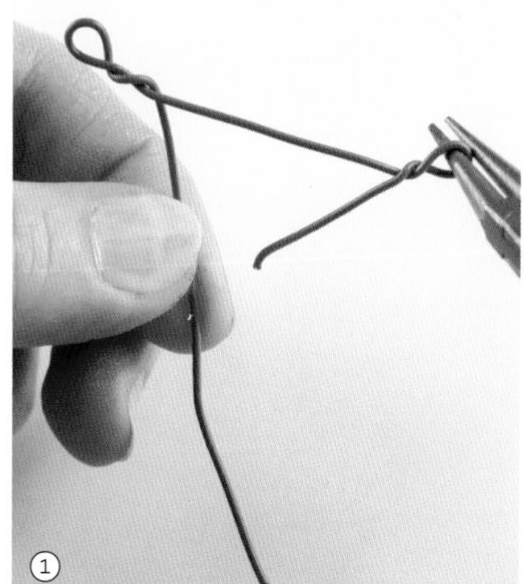

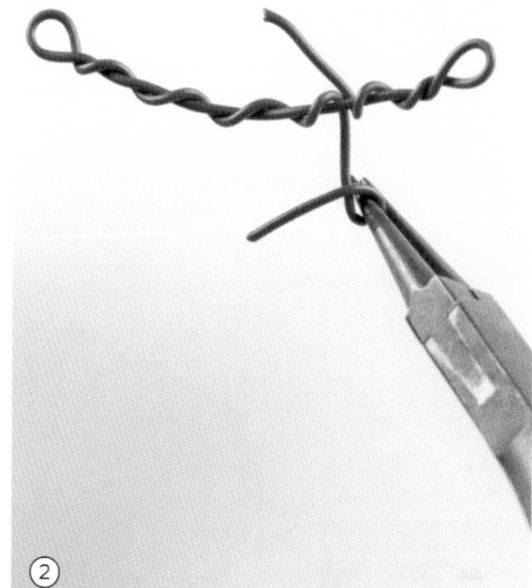

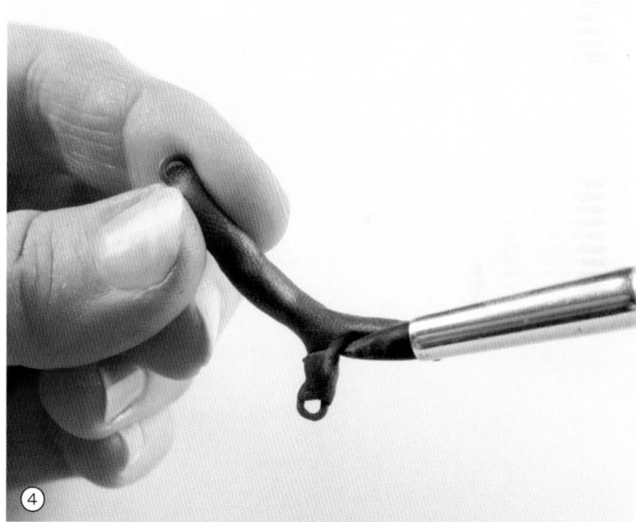

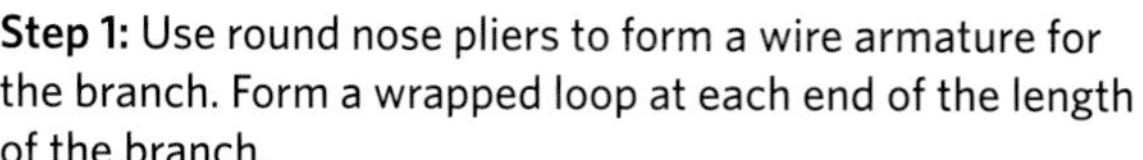

Step 1: Use round nose pliers to form a wire armature for the branch. Form a wrapped loop at each end of the length of the branch.

Step 2: Twist the wire toward the center to form a small twig with a loop. The twig will originate from the main branch.

Step 3: Roll a small snake of bronze or brown colored clay and wrap it over the wire armature to form the branch.

Step 4: Cover the small twig with clay and blend the clay seam into the main branch with a clay shaper tool. Score lines along the length of the branch to resemble bark.

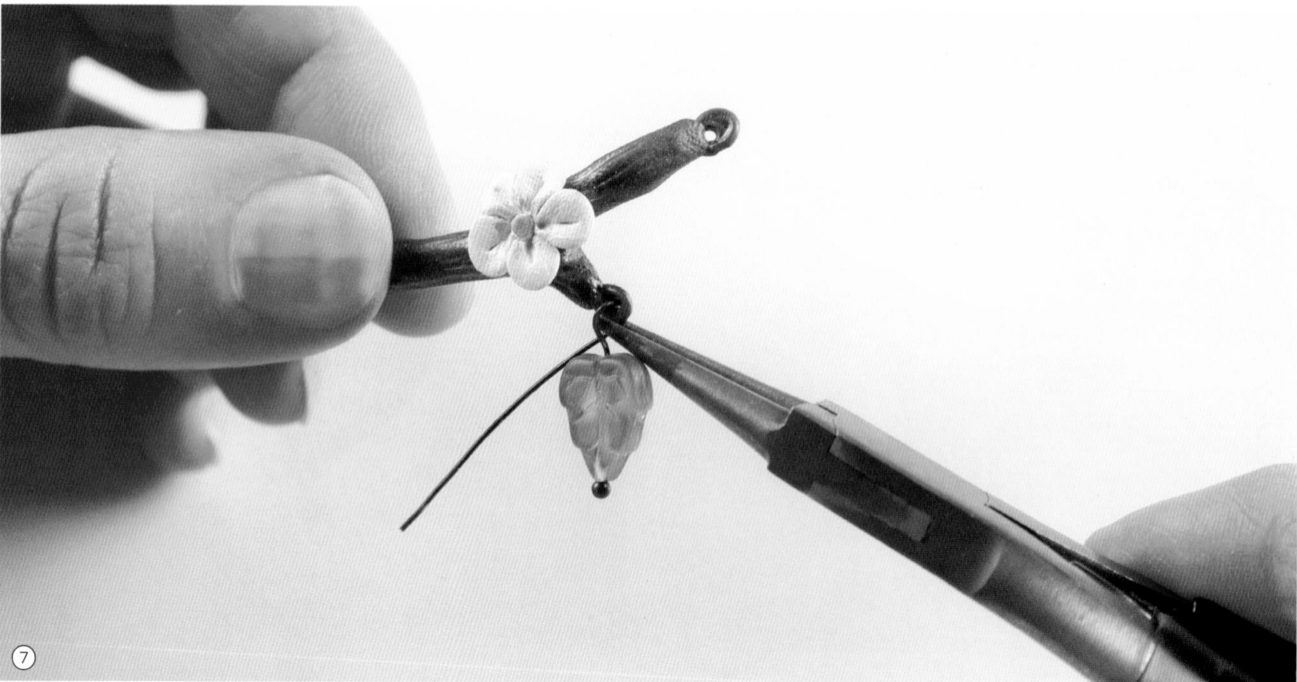

Step 5: Form a small flower with five tiny petal shapes using white clay. Use a clay shaper tool to press a depression in the branch for the flower placement. Press the center of the flower into the depression using a needle tool to attach the flower to the branch. Press a small ball of pink clay into the center of the flower.

Step 6: Bake the clay branch as directed for the clay you are using. After the branch is cool, paint the flower with accent colors (yellow was used in the center). Antique the branch with gold or bronze paint to highlight the bark texture. Paint the wire loops as well, if needed.

Step 7: Attach a glass leaf bead to the twig loop using a headpin. Pass the headpin through the bead and use the round nose pliers to form a loop at the top of the headpin to attach the bead to the twig. Wrap the base of the loop and clip off the excess wire.

HINT *You can prebake the flower for 10 minutes to preserve the form before you press it into the branch.*

FOR THE BRACELET

- 96 inches (244 cm) brown nylon bead cord, cut into 2 lengths of 48 inches (122 cm) each
- Small white faceted beads
- Thread burner tool

Step 1: Fold a 48 inch (122 cm) length of cord in half and attach to one of the loops at the end of the branch with a lark's head knot. Pull tightly. Begin tying three alternating half-hitch knots to start the bracelet pattern. Before tying the next knot, add a bead to that cord and loop the half-hitch under the bead, pulling tight. Tie three more alternating half-hitch knots and then add a bead to the cord next in line, pulling the half-hitch under the bead. Continue the pattern of three alternating half-hitch knots followed by a bead to complete half of the bracelet. Repeat the pattern on the other side with the remaining cord.

Step 2: When the pattern is complete on both sides, tie an overhand knot to finish each side. Use a small piece of leftover cord to tie an adjustable square knot slide as shown on page 41 to provide a closure. Add beads to the tail ends of the cords and finish with overhand knots. Use a thread burner tool to melt all of the cut cord ends, including the square knot slide ends, to keep them from unraveling.

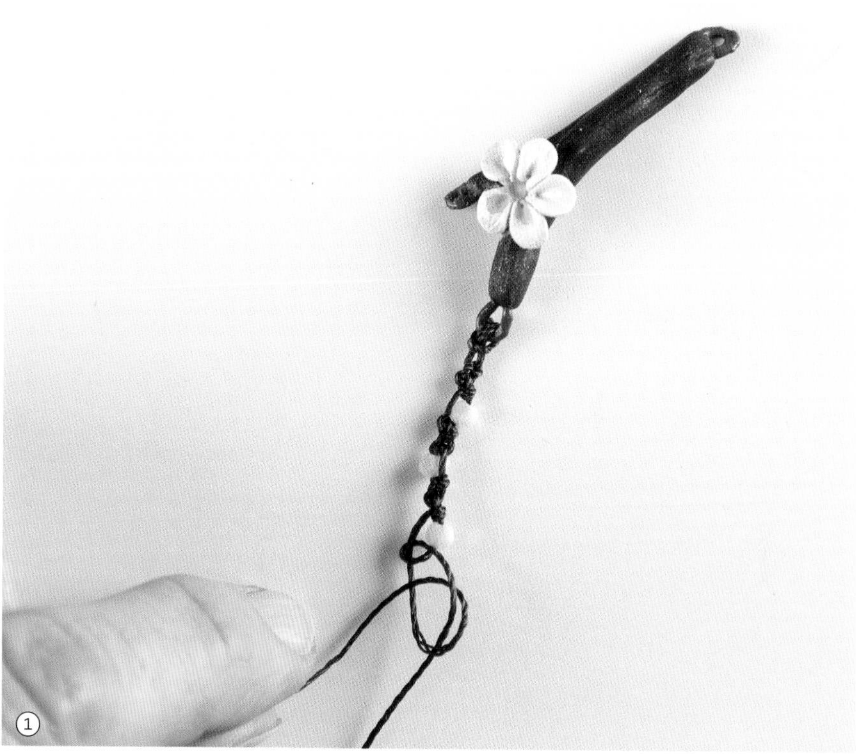
①

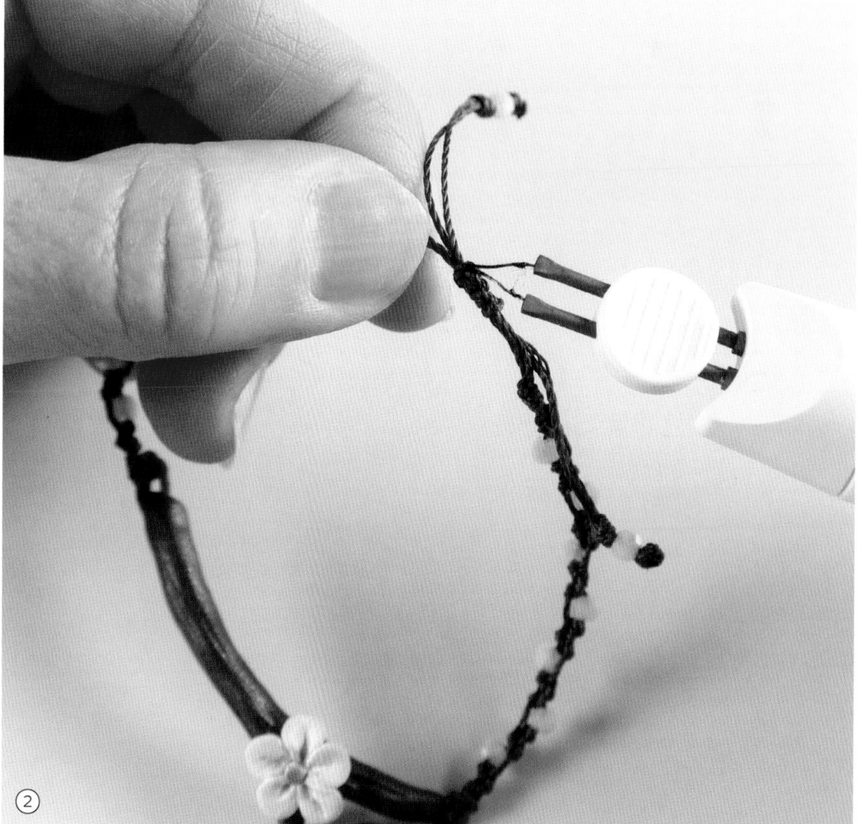
②

Green Glitterati

The charm featured in this bracelet uses polymer clay as a base for a mosaic of rhinestones and beads on a metal bezel. Make a symmetrical design like the one shown here or try an asymmetrical arrangement.

FOR THE CHARM

- Light green polymer clay
- Two round metal filigree findings
- Tweezers
- Glass rhinestones and seed beads
- Fine beading needle and fine thread or monofilament
- Two-part epoxy resin and toothpick
- Waxed paper

HINT *When choosing elements for your mosaic charm, only use items that are made of glass or other materials that can withstand the heat required to cure the clay; avoid plastic and any other materials that might melt or burn.*

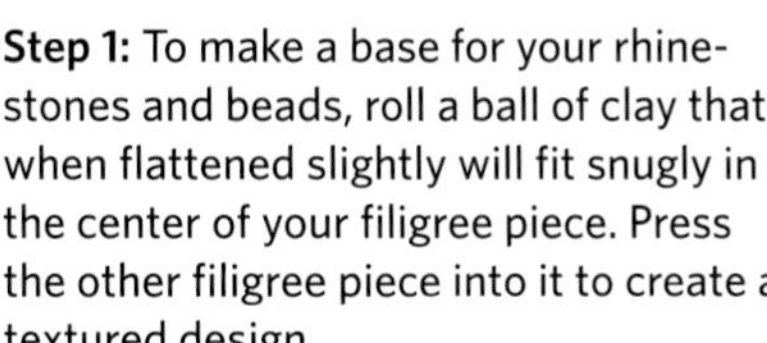

Step 1: To make a base for your rhinestones and beads, roll a ball of clay that when flattened slightly will fit snugly in the center of your filigree piece. Press the other filigree piece into it to create a textured design.

Step 2: Use tweezers to push rhinestones and seed beads into the clay. Carefully press the clay around the beads and stones to secure them. Bake according to the clay manufacturer's instructions. Let the clay cool completely.

Step 3: To frame the mosaic with a string of seed beads, use a beading wire to thread the beads on fine thread or monofilament. Wrap the beads around the clay to ensure that the string of beads wraps all the way around the clay. Attach the beads with epoxy resin to secure the beads close to the edge of the clay. Set the piece aside on waxed paper until the epoxy cures.

KNOTTING THE BRACELET

FOR THE BRACELET

Cotton embroidery floss in five colors—blue, violet, green, yellow, and orange—each 2 yards (1.8 m) long

Sewing needle

Strand of single rhinestones, 7 inches (18 cm) long

Scissors

This bracelet uses two knots—double half-hitch and lark's head—to form diagonal and diamond patterns. Always tie double half-hitch knots unless otherwise directed. The double half-hitches move across the work to form diagonal rows in the direction in which they're tied. The instructions specify when you'll need to tie lark's head knots, which will change the direction of the threads.

1

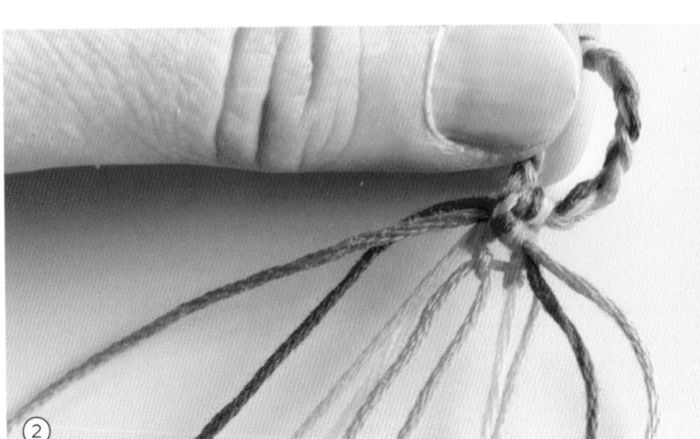
2

3

4

Step 1: Gather the five threads. Measure to the halfway point along their length and weave a three-strand braid (see page 25) for about 1¼ inches (3 cm) (one thread is worked on its own). Form a loop with the braided section and secure at the base with a square knot.

Step 2: Arrange the threads from left to right as follows: blue, violet, green, orange, yellow; yellow, orange, green, violet, blue. Working toward the center, tie the orange threads over each of the yellow threads and then tie the righthand orange thread over the lefthand orange thread. This sequence yields three knots: one in the center, with two above it on either side.

Step 3: Use the blue threads to tie a lark's head knot over the violet thread right next to each blue thread. You'll create single-color edges by keeping the blue threads on the outside and using them to tie lark's heads knots along the entire length of the bracelet *before starting every row.* The blue threads are *not* worked across the other threads.

Step 4: Working toward the center, tie the violet threads over each of the other threads and then tie the righthand violet thread over the lefthand one. Tie lark's head knots with the blue threads over the threads that are now next to them (green) before starting the next row.

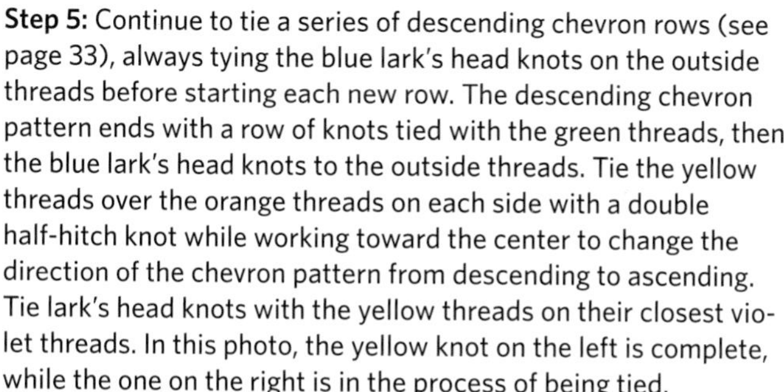

Step 5: Continue to tie a series of descending chevron rows (see page 33), always tying the blue lark's head knots on the outside threads before starting each new row. The descending chevron pattern ends with a row of knots tied with the green threads, then the blue lark's head knots to the outside threads. Tie the yellow threads over the orange threads on each side with a double half-hitch knot while working toward the center to change the direction of the chevron pattern from descending to ascending. Tie lark's head knots with the yellow threads on their closest violet threads. In this photo, the yellow knot on the left is complete, while the one on the right is in the process of being tied.

Step 6: Tie each of the blue threads to the outside threads with a lark's head knot. Working from the center out, tie the yellow threads on the orange threads with double half-hitch knots.

Step 7: Once again, start a row by tying each of the blue threads to the outside threads with a lark's head knot. Working with the green threads from the center out, tie a diagonal row on both sides and then tie each of the blue threads to the green threads with a lark's head knot. In this photo, the left side of the row is complete and the right side is in process.

Step 8: Working from the center outward, tie three rows of double half-hitch knots, making sure to tie the blue threads to the outside threads with a lark's head knot before starting each one. Begin at the center by tying a knot with threads of the same color. Keep working down both sides as you did in the previous step. End with a yellow row. To form a diamond, start in the center with a green double half-hitch. Working toward the outside, tie double half-hitches on the violet threads and then tie lark's head knots on the orange threads, which will turn the direction of the knots back toward the middle. Use the two violet threads to tie a double half-hitch in the center.

Step 9: Tie each of the blue threads to the outside threads with a lark's head knot. Working toward the center, tie a row of green threads with double half-hitches, finishing with a knot in the center. Repeat, this time using the yellow threads to tie a row of double half-hitch knots.

Step 10: Finish in the center with a knot. Tie each of the blue threads to the outside (orange) threads with a lark's head knot and then continue tying the orange threads toward the center. Return to step 4 to repeat the chevron pattern.

Step 11: Continue to knot the pattern until the bracelet is long enough to fit your wrist. (Be sure to include the knotted loop closure in your measurement.) Make ties by dividing the threads into two sections and braiding each in a three-strand braid (page 25). Knot the end of each braid and trim the excess threads.

Step 12: Sew the charm to the center front of the bracelet and then stitch a strand of rhinestones along its center length on either side of the charm. Knot and weave in the thread ends on the back of the bracelet.

VARIATION

Chain Reaction

In this design, which follows the same basic instructions as for Green Glitterati, the clay mosaic is surrounded with a strand of tiny single rhinestones, and a metal curb chain is woven in on both sides of the bracelet.

FOR THE CHARM

- Orange polymer clay
- Two round metal filigree findings
- Tweezers
- Glass rhinestones and seed beads
- Strand of single glass rhinestones, 7 inches (18 cm) long
- Two-part epoxy resin and toothpick
- Waxed paper

FOR THE BRACELET

- Cotton embroidery floss in five colors—red, orange, green, white, and blue—each 2 yards (1.8 m) long
- Two lengths of metal curb chain in gold, each about 7 inches (18 cm) long
- Scissors

HINT *The two pieces of curb chain that are used to embellish the edges of the bracelet should be cut to fit snugly around your wrist. The knotted closure will increase the overall finished length of the bracelet.*

MAKING THE CHARMS

2

Step 1: Following steps 1 through 3 for Making the Charm on page 65, make a mosaic charm using orange clay and glass rhinestones and seed beads.

Step 2: Cure the charm according to the clay manufacturer's instructions. Then frame it with a strand of glass rhinestones, using epoxy resin to secure it around the edge. Let it cure undisturbed on a piece of waxed paper.

KNOTTING THE BRACELET

This bracelet follows the same basic knotting pattern as the Green Glitterati bracelet on page 64.

1

2

Step 1: Follow steps 1 through 12 for Green Glitterati on pages 66 through 68, using colors specified on page 69. After finishing the braided closure with a square knot, arrange the colors in this order: red, orange, green, white, blue; blue, white, green, orange, red. To add the chain along each edge, pass the outside (red) threads of the first full chevron row up though a chain link on either side and then tie a lark's head on the thread next to it. The red threads should remain on the outside of the bracelet and are *not* worked across. The first loop of the lark's head knot is shown here, being tied around the orange thread.

Step 2: Continue working the same knotting pattern as for Green Glitterati, remembering to thread the red thread up through a chain link and tie a lark's head knot to the thread beside it before starting each row.

Step 3: When you've reached the end of the chain, make ties by dividing the threads into two sections and braiding each in a three-strand braid (page 25). Knot the end of each braid and trim the excess threads. Sew the charm to the front of the bracelet and then knot and weave in the thread end on the back.

Forever Yours

The infinity symbol is a mathematical symbol representing the concept of infinity. The shape appears as a sideways number 8 and is a popular symbol for jewelry design. Since this is a delicate design to make with polymer clay, the shape is reinforced with wire inside for strength. Personalize the symbol with rhinestones or crystals in the color of your birthstone.

MAKING THE CHARM

FOR THE CHARM

- 18-gauge copper or brass wire 10 inches (25.5 cm) long
- White polymer clay with glitter, such as FIMO
- Three small glass rhinestones in birthstone color of choice
- Wooden spoon, pen, or other rounded form
- Clay shaper or sculpting tool
- Heavy-duty household pliers

①

②

③

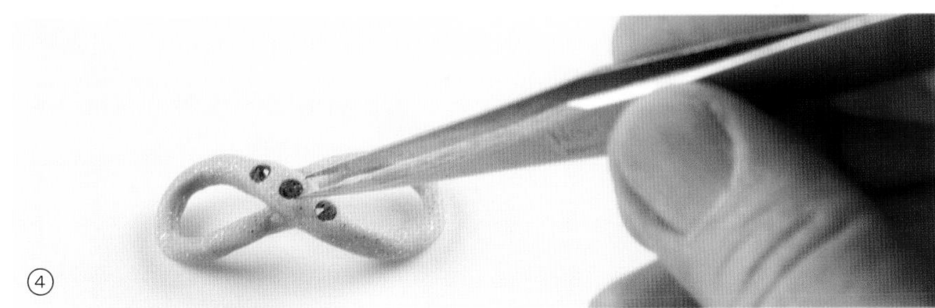
④

Step 1: Bend the wire into the shape of a figure 8 using a rounded form such as a wooden spoon handle or pen to shape the wire. Bend the ends of the wire in the center as shown to secure the shape. Use heavy-duty pliers to crimp down on the wire bends to flatten them. Shape the wire to form a slight curve over your wrist.

Step 2: Roll out a narrow snake of clay to use to cover the wire. Flatten the snake and wrap the clay around the wire figure 8.

Step 3: Blend the seams of the clay over the wire and smooth the surface of the clay, taking care to bury and hide the wire inside.

Step 4: Add more clay to the center of the figure 8, building it up so that it has a dimensional over-under look. Use a sculpting tool to help you shape the clay. Press three glass rhinestones into the clay for more sparkle. Bake the clay-covered wire for 30 minutes.

FOR THE BRACELET

- 6 yards (5.5 m) embroidery floss, cut into six 1-yard (1 m) lengths
- Six crystal beads
- White glue
- Toothpick

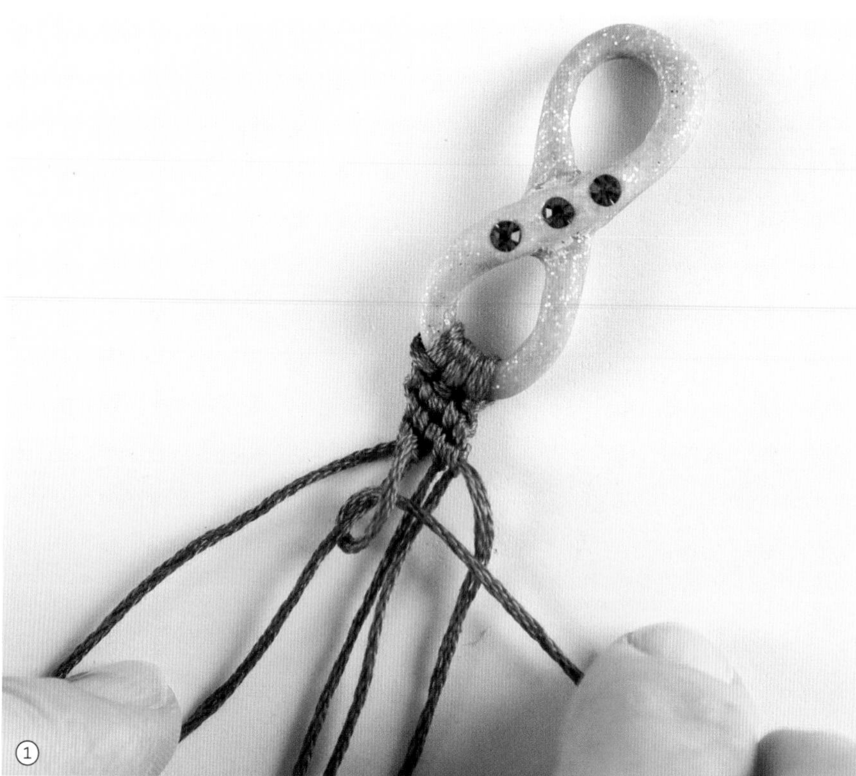

①

Step 1: Double each of the threads and attach three threads to each side of the infinity clay centerpiece, attaching each with a lark's head knot as shown on page 31. This will give you six threads with which to tie diagonal double half-hitch knots across with width of the bracelet. Start with the thread on the left and tie it over each thread in the row using a double half-hitch knot. When one row is complete, start with the next thread and work from left to right. See page 32 for the instructions for the diagonal double half-hitch pattern. Use this pattern for both sides of the bracelet.

Step 2: Finish by securing the threads with an overhand knot. Leave tails to tie the bracelet on with. Embellish with crystal beads tied on with overhand knots. Apply white glue close to the beads to prevent the thread from fraying.

②

California Dreaming

This Boho-chic, wrap-style bracelet conjures up images of a beach cafe on a warm summer's evening. The colors and shapes of the rose and leaf charms are inspired by richly painted mid-century California pottery.

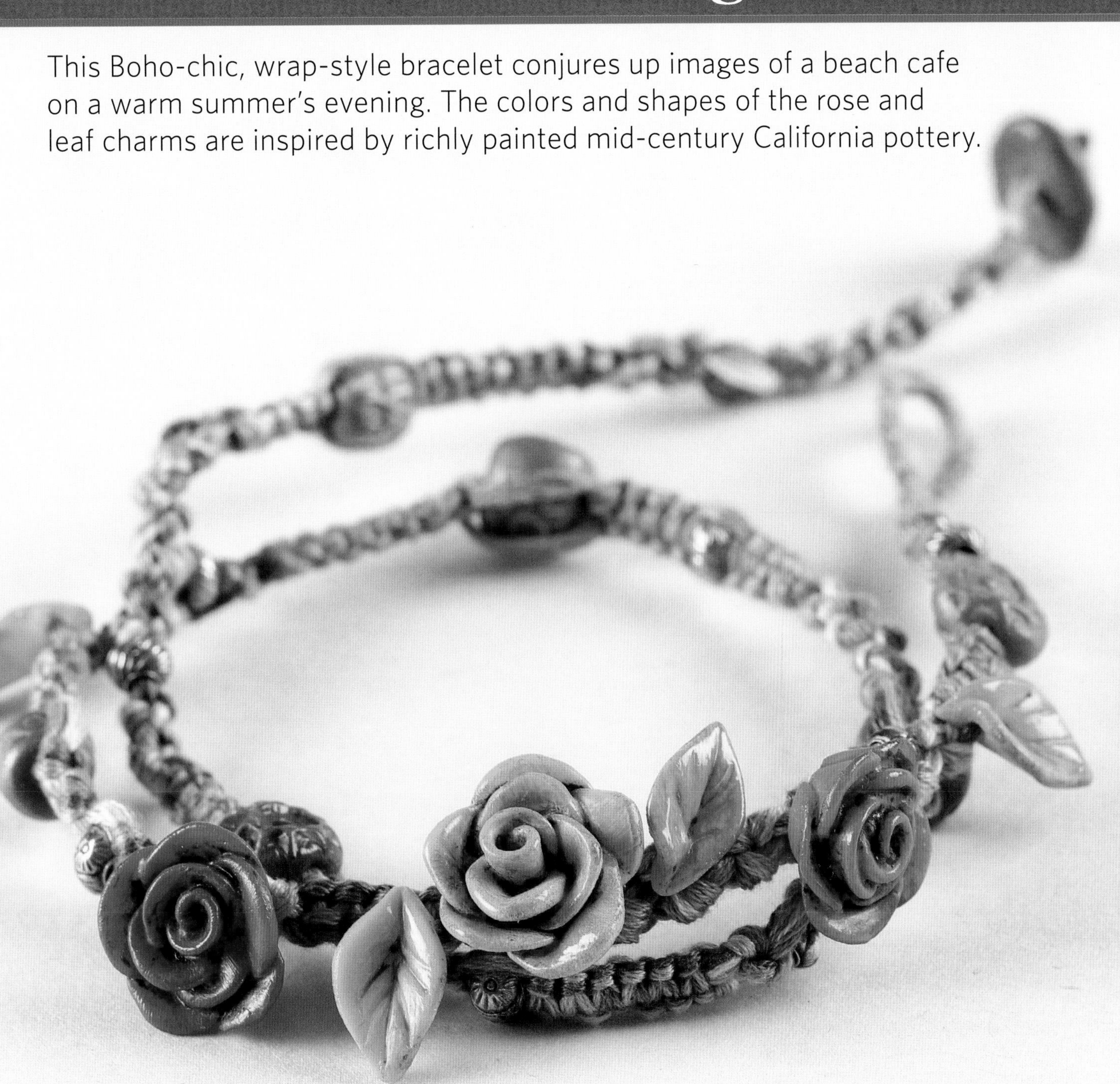

FOR THE CHARMS AND BEADS

- Polymer clay in orange, yellow, and red for the roses and leaves; blue and green for the beads
- Craft knife or mat cutter blade
- Plastic-coated wire in red
- Two-part epoxy resin (for securing wire shanks, as needed) and toothpick
- Waxed paper
- Needle tool
- Rubber stamp texture sheets
- Liquid polymer clay
- Embossing heat tool
- Acrylic paint or antiquing medium in brown
- Paintbrush
- Paper towel
- Gilders paste

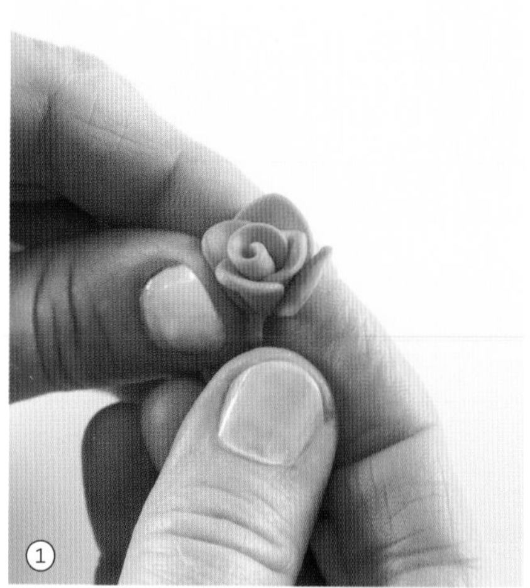

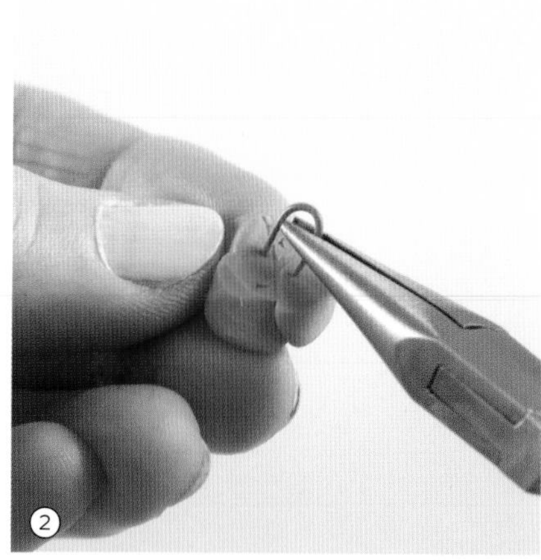

Making the Rose Charms

Step 1: To make the rose charms, form petals by flattening tiny balls of clay into slightly pointed ovals. Make five to nine petals for each rose, depending on how large you want them to be. Roll one of the petals into a coil to make the center and then press the other petals around it, overlapping them as you go.

Step 2: After the rose is formed, use a craft knife or mat cutter blade to slice off excess clay from the back to make it flat. Bend a small piece of plastic-coated wire and embed it into the back of the rose to create a shank through which to pass the threads. Bake the roses according to the manufacturer's instructions with the wires in place. Test the wires after the roses have cooled completely, using epoxy resin to secure any that can be pulled out.

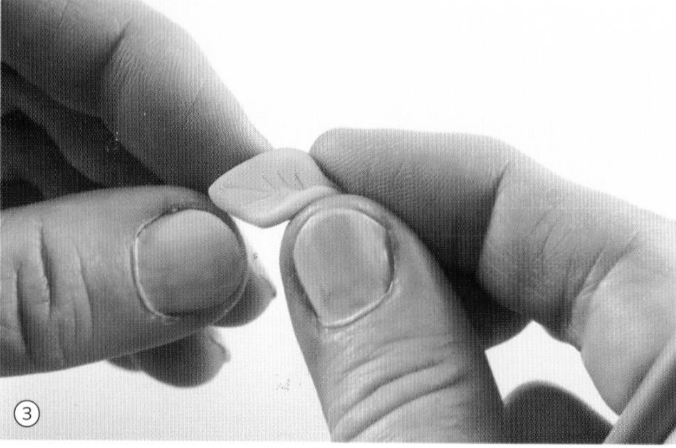

Making the Leaf Charms

Step 3: To make leaf charms, form small, flat teardrop shapes and then use a needle tool to score vein lines into each one.

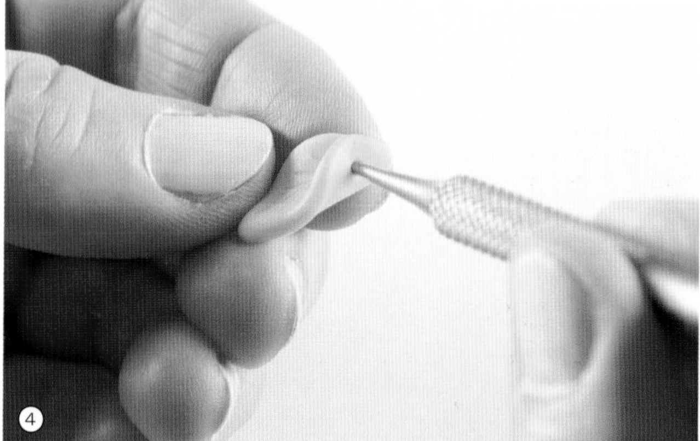

Step 4: Pinch the base of each leaf and then use a needle tool to pierce a hole sideways through the pinched area as shown. Make sure the hole is large enough to thread two strands of floss through.

⑤

⑥

⑦

Making the Textured Beads

Step 5: To make textured beads, roll balls of clay and press each one into a texture sheet. (Texture both sides of the bead at once by pressing it with a second sheet.) Make a button for the closure by texturing a flattened oval. Before curing, pierce a hole through the sides of each bead and two holes through the top of the flat oval button.

Step 6: Make cylinder-shaped beads by piercing a ball of clay with a needle tool and rolling the side of it over a texture sheet.

Step 7: To finish the beads, cure according to the clay manufacturer's instructions. Let them cool completely. Apply a coat of liquid polymer clay to the rose and leaf charms and then cure them with an embossing heat tool according to the clay manufacturer's instructions. (The liquid clay will turn clear fairly quickly, so take care not to burn it.) Once cool, apply acrylic paint or antiquing medium to the roses, leaves, and textured beads and then wipe off with a slightly dampened paper towel. Once the paint or gel is dry, apply highlights sparingly to the textured beads with gilders paste.

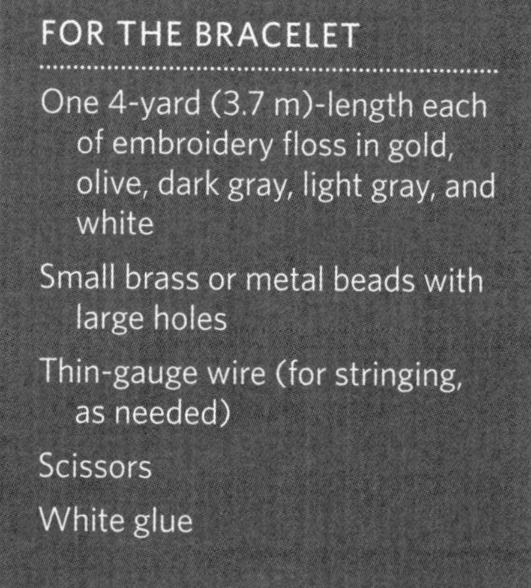

FOR THE BRACELET

One 4-yard (3.7 m)-length each of embroidery floss in gold, olive, dark gray, light gray, and white

Small brass or metal beads with large holes

Thin-gauge wire (for stringing, as needed)

Scissors

White glue

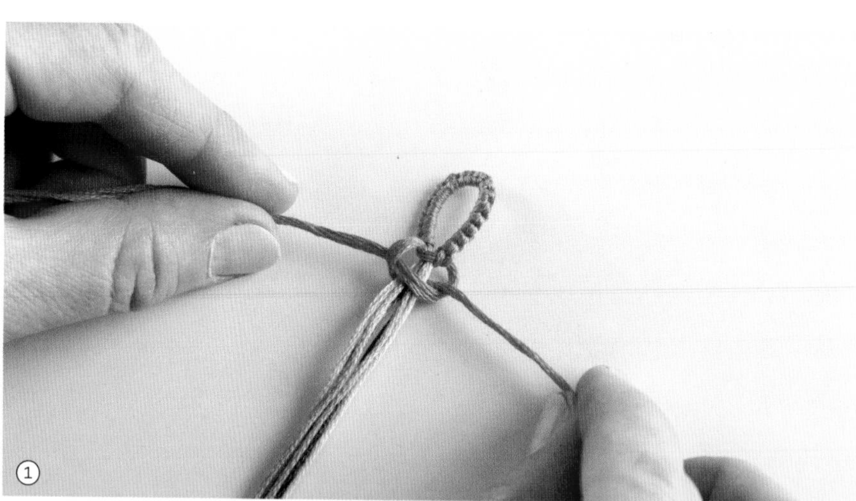

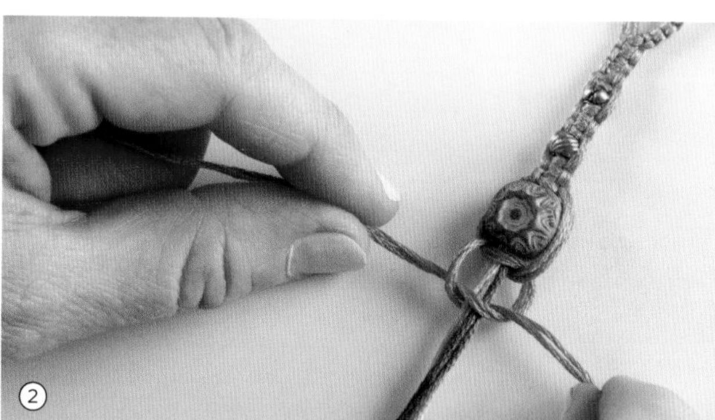

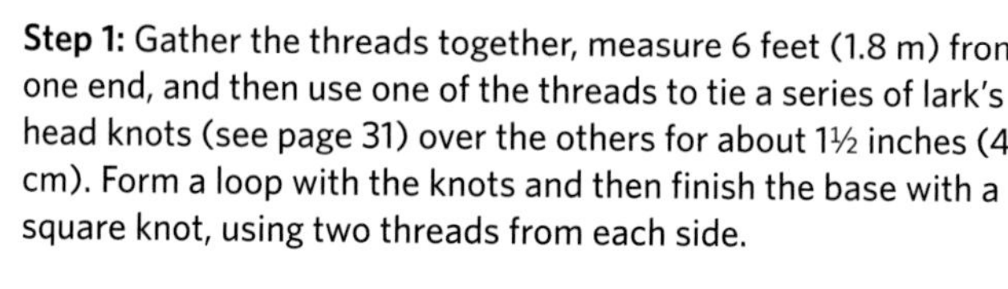

Step 1: Gather the threads together, measure 6 feet (1.8 m) from one end, and then use one of the threads to tie a series of lark's head knots (see page 31) over the others for about 1½ inches (4 cm). Form a loop with the knots and then finish the base with a square knot, using two threads from each side.

Step 2: Continue the pattern by tying square knots. Using the same two threads on each side, add metal accent beads and a textured bead every ½ inch (1.3 cm), alternating them and tying square knots under each. If needed, use a bent piece of thin-gauge wire to help thread the beads over the core threads.

Step 3: To change the knot pattern, separate the threads into two sections with five threads each. Tie a series of alternating half-hitch knots (see page 30), adding leaf and rose charms as you go, passing a few of the threads through the beads' holes or wire shanks. Continue adding charms and beads along the way as desired, alternating sequences of square knots with half-hitch knots every 2 to 3 inches (5 to 7.5 cm), working until the bracelet is long enough to wrap around your wrist two or three times.

Step 4: To add the button for the closure, divide the threads into two sections and thread each through one of the holes. Tie the thread ends with a square knot at the top of the button, trim the excess, and seal the knot with glue.

Cityscape

One great thing about working with polymer clay is that it has the ability to imitate a lot of materials. The look of a rough concrete surface can be achieved by rolling sand and glitter onto a clay surface. This bracelet design is simple and neutral in color, perfect for a minimalist, contemporary look.

MAKING THE CHARM

FOR THE CHARM

Gray polymer clay
Black sand
Glitter (glass or silver color)
Small piece of rhinestone chain
Clay roller
Craft knife
Needle tool
Ceramic mug

1

2

3

Step 1: Roll out a thick sheet of gray colored clay. To make the surface look like concrete, sprinkle black sand and silver or glass glitter onto the surface and roll over the clay to embed the sand.

Step 2: Press a small length of rhinestone chain into the clay.

Step 3: Cut a thin rectangle strip around the rhinestones to make the bracelet centerpiece the desired length. Use the needle tool to pierce a hole on each side for stringing. Tip a ceramic mug on its side and drape the strip of clay across the side of the mug to give the clay a curved shape. Use leftover clay to make two small clay beads to add to the ends of the finished bracelet cords. Bake the pieces according to the clay manufacturer's instructions and allow to cool before refining the holes with the tip of a craft knife, if needed.

FOR THE BRACELET

80 inches (203 cm) black nylon bead cord

Scissors

Thread burner tool or glue

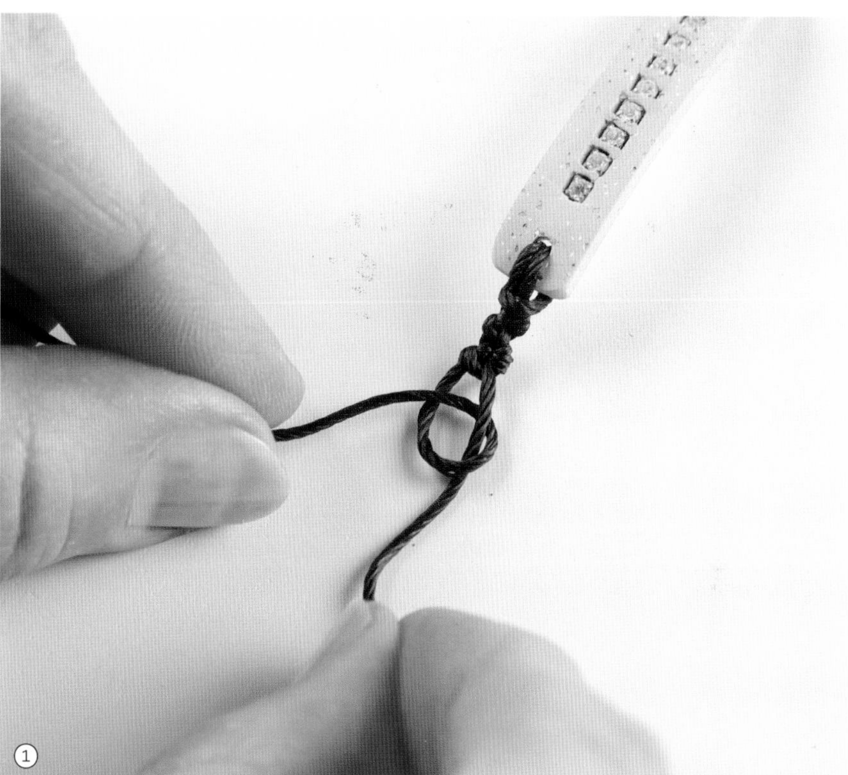

1

Step 1: Cut two 40 inch (101.5 cm) long pieces of nylon cord, one for each side of the bracelet. Double one of the cords and loop it through one of the holes on the clay strip with a lark's head knot. This will give you two threads with which to knot. Use an alternating half-hitch pattern to knot one side of the bracelet. Attach the remaining cord and knot to complete the other side.

Step 2: Add the small clay beads to the ends of the cords. Finish with overhand knots to secure the beads. Use a thread burner tool to melt the cord ends close to the knots for a nice, neat finish. Alternatively, you can use glue to seal the knots. Simply tie the cords to fasten on your wrist or add an adjustable square knot closure as shown on page 80.

2

VARIATION

Button Up

A clay button doubles as the featured centerpiece and a clever closure for a knotted design. To make a clay button for a loop closure, make sure the button shape fits through the loop on the other end of the bracelet, but be careful not to make it too small. This design features a contemporary style button using gray polymer clay to simulate concrete.

FOR THE BUTTON

- Gray polymer clay
- Black sand
- Glitter (glass or silver color)
- Loose glass rhinestones
- Needle tool
- Clay roller

FOR THE BRACELET

- 70 inches (177.8 cm) black nylon bead cord
- Scissors
- Thread burner tool

MAKING THE BUTTON

Step 1: Roll a small ball of gray clay and flatten it to make a button shape. Press sand and glitter onto the surface as directed for the Cityscape project on page 78. Press glass rhinestones into the surface of the clay and use a needle tool to form a hole in the center of the button.

Step 2: Bake the clay button according to the clay manufacturer's instructions and cool.

KNOTTING THE BRACELET

1

2

Step 1: To string the bracelet, cut two pieces of nylon bead cord. Cut one piece 40 inches (101.5 cm) long and the other 30 inches (76 cm) long. Hold the cords even at one end and measure down about 28 inches (71 cm) to begin tying a lark's head loop that will serve as the closure. Tie the longer cord over the shorter one (core) to form a row of lark's head knots. Tie enough knots so that the row of knots will fit snugly over the button when formed into a loop. (See page 39 for how to create this type of closure.) When the length is sufficient, gather the cord ends to form the loop. You will have four strands of cord. Begin weaving the bracelet with a four-strand braid pattern (see page 26).

Step 2: When the bracelet is long enough to fit around your wrist, pass the ends of all four cords through the center hole of the clay button. Tie an overhand knot to secure the cords on the front side of the button. Clip the ends of the cords close to the knot and seal by melting the cord ends with a thread burner tool.

Faceted Fragments

The rich-toned colors of the beads in this bracelet design represent the ancient classical elements of earth, wind, fire, and air. To enhance the organic look of the beads, bits of dried or baked clay are mixed in to create a faux stone or granite texture before shaping and cutting. For a bold, minimalist statement, make a bracelet that features a single large bead.

FOR THE BEADS

- Polymer clay in turquoise, red, green, and yellow
- Dried or cured clay
- Craft knife or mat cutter blade
- Short length of heavy-gauge wire
- Baking tray
- Black colored pencil
- Polymer clay varnish, matte or gloss
- Paintbrush

①

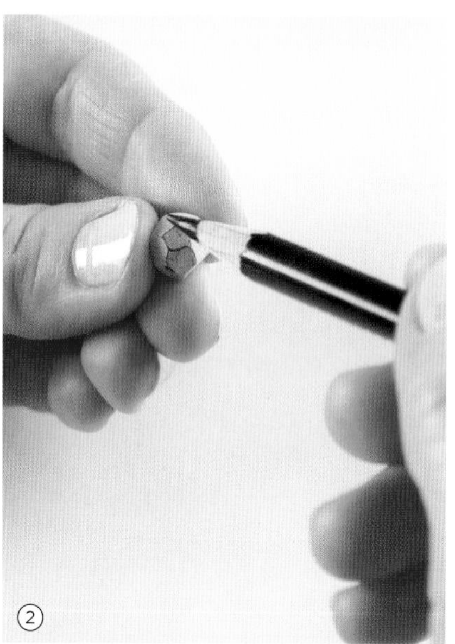

②

③

④

Step 1: To make each bead, roll a small ball of clay and then roll it in bits of dried or cured clay. Refrigerate or freeze the beads for at least 30 minutes to firm them up. Create facets by slicing off small areas around the entire surface of each bead with a craft knife or mat cutter blade.

Step 2: Use a wire to pierce the beads, making sure the holes are large enough to fit all four strands of the thread that will be used to make the bracelet. Slide the beads onto the wire, suspend the wire over a baking tray, and bake according to the clay manufacturer's instructions. Let the beads cool completely.

Step 3: Use a black colored pencil to emphasize the edges of the facets. Seal the pencil with polymer clay varnish.

Step 4: Leave the beads on the wire until the varnish is completely dry.

FOR THE BRACELET

Two lengths of waxed linen thread, one 48 inches (122 cm) and one 60 inches (152 cm)

Short length of fine-gauge wire

White glue

Step 1: To create a loop closure at the end of the bracelet, measure 23 inches (58 cm) from the end of each length of thread and then use the longer thread to tie about 1¼ inches (3 cm) of lark's head knots around the shorter one (the core).

Step 2: With the knots, form a loop to fit snuggly over one of the beads to create a buttonhole closure. Gather the threads at the base. Four threads will extend down from the loop. Tie a square knot by tying the two outside threads around the two at the center. Pull tightly to secure the base of the loop.

Step 3: Braid the threads using the four-strand braid pattern (see page 26) until you're ready to add beads. (For the sample bracelets shown on page 81, we braided the threads for about 3 inches [7.5 cm] before adding multiple beads in various colors.)

Step 4: Tie an overhand knot (see page 25) with all four threads just before adding the beads, stringing them over all four threads. Use the fine-gauge wire to aid with threading if needed. Tie another overhand knot after threading the last bead.

Step 5: Continue braiding as in step 3 until the bracelet fits around your wrist. (Be sure to include the knotted loop closure in your measurement.) Tie an overhand knot, add a bead for the closure, and finish with another overhand knot. Secure all of the cut thread ends with glue to keep them from unraveling.

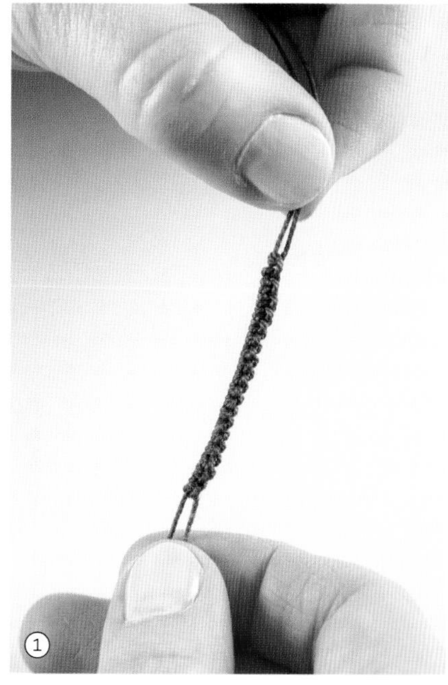
1

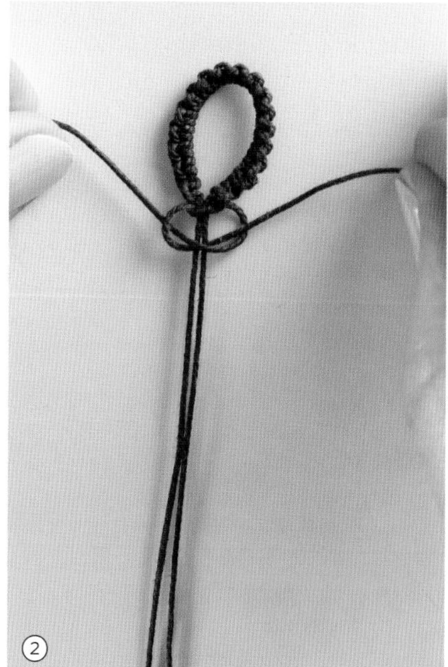
2

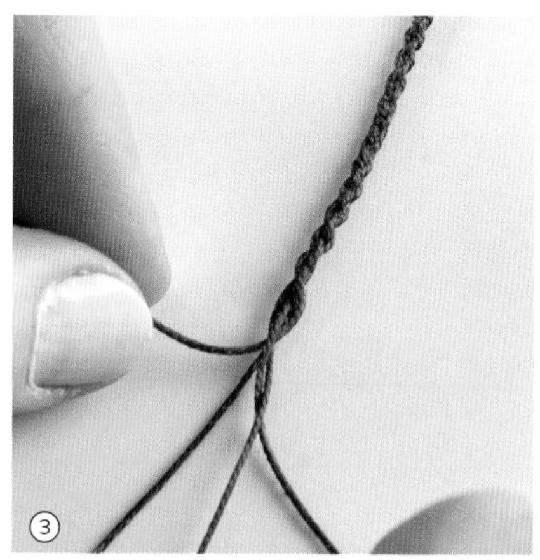
3

4

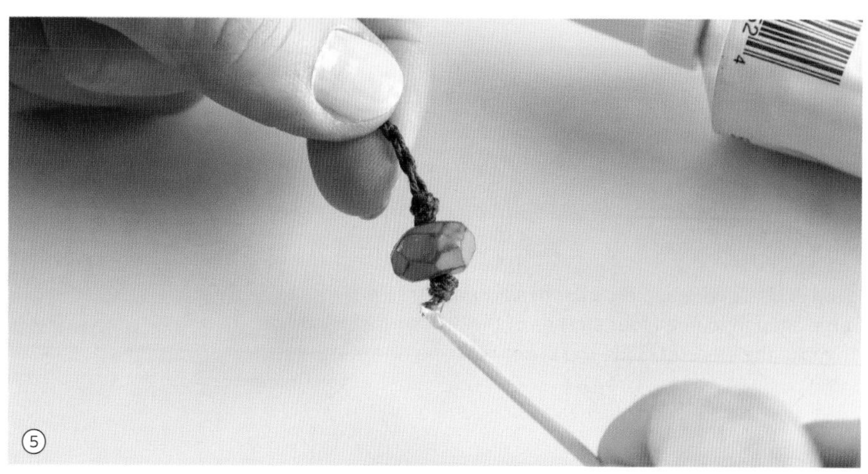
5

Bronze Angel

A gold foil Dresden die-cut wing was used to create a mold for this project. Dresden die cuts originated in Germany and have been produced since the early nineteenth century. Some continue to be stamped from original press molds today. The die cuts are dimensional and provide nice detail when molded. Dresden wing shapes are available through online retailers or from vintage paper suppliers.

FOR THE CHARM

- German Dresden foil wing
- Two-part silicone mold putty
- Bronze polymer clay
- Assortment of metallic acrylic paint colors
- Paintbrush
- Craft knife
- Needle tool
- Ceramic mug
- Paper towel

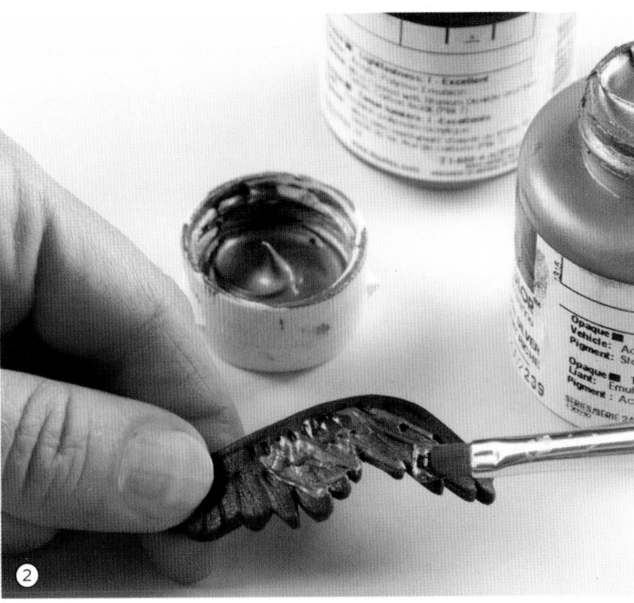

Step 1: To create a mold of a Dresden foil wing shape, prepare the two-part silicone mold putty according to the manufacturer's instructions and press the wing into the putty. Let the putty cure and remove the wing. Press the conditioned polymer clay into the mold to cast a wing relief. Roll over the back to flatten and remove from the mold. Trim off the edges with a craft knife and use a needle or sculpting tool to refine and add detail. Pierce a hole at each end of the wing.

Step 2: Drape the wing over the side of a tipped over oven-safe ceramic mug to form it into a curve. Bake the wing on the mug for 30 minutes according to the clay manufacturer's instructions. Paint the surface of the wing with metallic acrylic paint colors to emphasize the details.

Step 3: While the paint is still wet, wipe off the surface with a damp paper towel. Let the paint dry.

FOR THE BRACELET

- 9 yards (8.2 m) nylon bead cord, cut into 4 pieces, 80 inches (203 cm) long each
- Pin vise with small drill bit or craft knife
- Assorted small beads (brass, rhinestone, or other material)
- Lobster claw clasp
- Thread burner tool or glue

Step 1: Double each cord and attach two cords to each side of the wing using lark's head knots. Use a drill or knife to enlarge the holes on the wing so they are large enough to accommodate two cords. This will give you four cords to work with on each side: two cords will serve as the core cords while the other two are used for tying. For the bracelet pattern, tie a combination of alternating lark's head knots with square knots. Tie a pattern of six alternating lark's head knots, as shown on page 31, followed by square knots and beads.

Step 2: Tie a square knot before and after the addition of each bead along the pattern. Keep tying knots, adding beads along the way on both sides of the wing. When the cords are long enough to wrap twice around your wrist, tie a clasp to the end of one side with an overhand knot. Secure the knot with a thread burner tool or with glue. Tie a loop of thread on the other end of the bracelet for attaching the clasp.

White-Winged Dove

Create a frosty white variation of the bronze wing bracelet using white pearl polymer clay with silver thread and beads. This bracelet features a spiral knotted pattern embellished with small silver beads. As a symbol, the wing represents the power of thought, rising above adversity, healing, and renewal, just to name a few. Whether or not meaning is assigned, the wing is a classic image in the jewelry design tradition.

FOR THE CHARM

- White pearl polymer clay
- Antiquing medium or brown acrylic paint
- Wing mold (see Bronze Angel project)
- Paintbrush
- Knife
- Needle tool
- Ceramic mug
- Paper towel

FOR THE BRACELET

- 120 inches (305 cm) light gray nylon bead cord, cut into two pieces measuring 60 inches (152.5 cm) each
- Silver beads
- Thread burner tool or glue

MAKING THE CHARMS

Follow the steps to make a clay wing as directed in the Bronze Angel project, page 85. After baking the clay, paint the recessed areas with antiquing medium or acrylic paint. Wipe the excess paint from the surface and allow to dry.

KNOTTING THE BRACELET

Step 1: To thread the bracelet, fold each cord at 12 inches (30.5 cm), leaving 48 inches (122 cm) with which to knot. Attach a cord through the holes on the wing using a lark's head knot as shown on page 31.

Step 2: Tie a series of spiral half-hitch knots with the longer cord, adding beads along the way. Pass both cords through the beads as you go. Finish both sides, working until the bracelet is long enough to fit your wrist. Secure the cords with overhand knots to finish. Leave tails of the cord for tying the bracelet. Add beads to the ends of the cord with overhand knots. Clip off the excess cord. Use a thread burner tool or glue to seal the ends of the knots.

Love Letters

Stamp a sentiment on these cheery hearts. Letter stamps were used to stamp "Love" in different languages on these polymer heart beads. Other ideas include stamping a friend's name or a favorite quote to personalize a lovely charm bracelet. The beads are decorated with pencils and marking pens. Use good quality art materials that are rich with pigments for best results.

FOR THE CHARMS

- White polymer clay
- Plastic coated wire for loops
- Metal letter and texture stamps
- Wire-plastic coated or metal
- Art marker pens
- Colored pencils
- Cotton swabs
- Rubbing alcohol
- Antiquing medium or acrylic paint (black or dark brown)
- Paper towel
- Polymer clay varnish
- Paintbrush

①

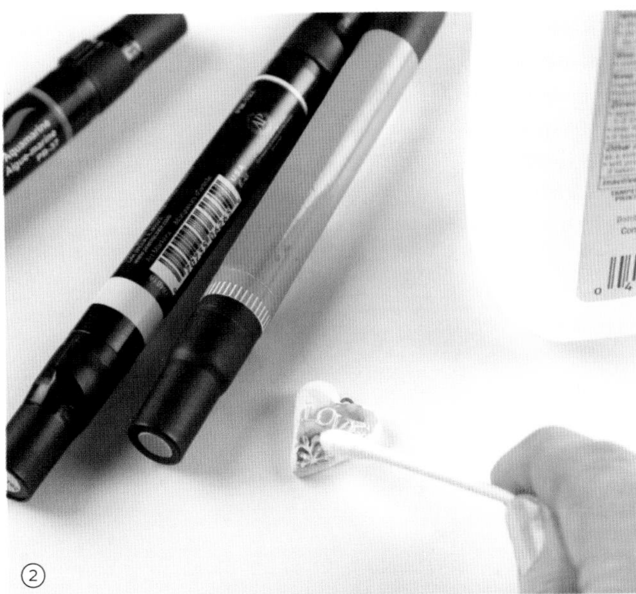

②

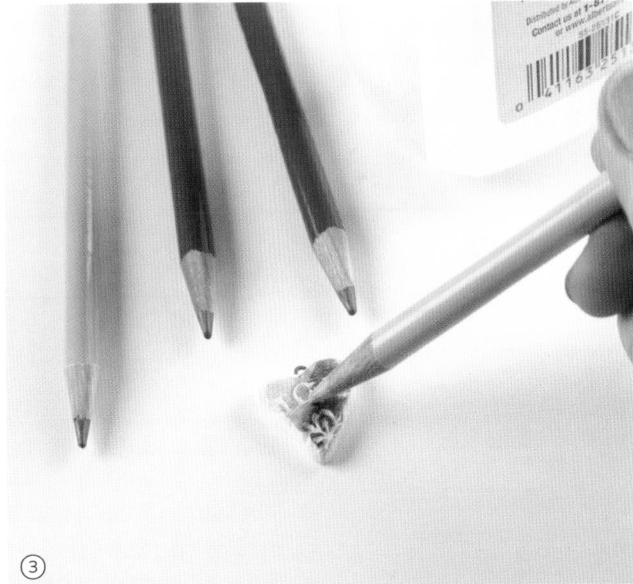

③

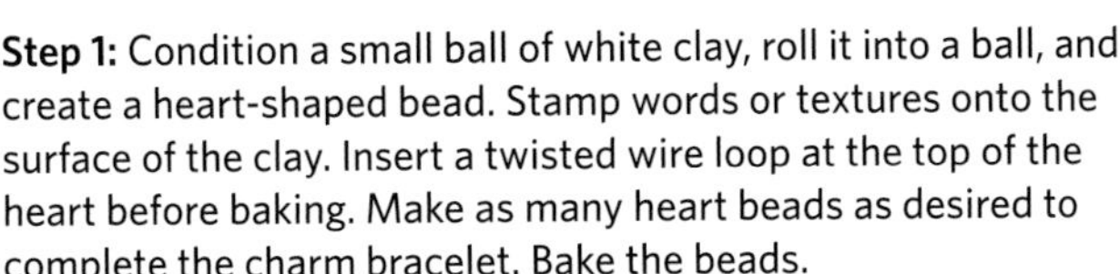

Step 1: Condition a small ball of white clay, roll it into a ball, and create a heart-shaped bead. Stamp words or textures onto the surface of the clay. Insert a twisted wire loop at the top of the heart before baking. Make as many heart beads as desired to complete the charm bracelet. Bake the beads.

Step 2: Add color to the beads with markers. Use cotton swabs and rubbing alcohol to blend the colors as desired.

Step 3: Layer colored pencil over the markers to add more depth to the design. Finish by rubbing acrylic paint or antiquing medium into the recessed textures. Wipe off the excess paint with a paper towel. After the paint is dry, seal the surface with a polymer clay varnish.

FOR THE BRACELET

- Curb chain for bracelet (cut to fit your wrist)
- Five threads of embroidery floss, each cut to a length of 1 yard (1 m)
- Fine wire for threading
- Jump rings
- Head pins
- Glass beads
- Lobster claw clasp
- Pliers
- Scissors

①

②

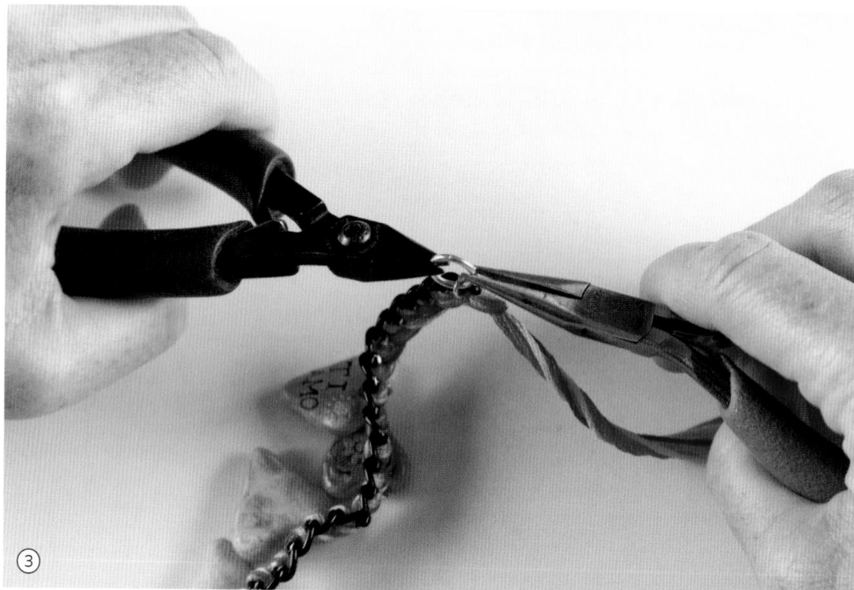
③

Step 1: Knot the embroidery floss at one end of the bracelet chain. Leave a small tail of threads at the end of the bracelet. Tie one half-hitch knot through each link, working down one side of the curb chain with the threads. Use a fine wire to thread the floss through the chain.

Step 2: Pull the threads through each link. Knot the thread to the last link to finish. Cut off the excess thread.

Step 3: Use the pliers to attach the hearts along the knotted threads with jump rings. Add a clasp to one end and a large jump ring to the other side. Attach the beads to head pins and add to the thread work.

Into the Woods

This bracelet design celebrates the magic and wonder of favorite childhood fairy tales. Look through vintage illustrated fairy tale books for inspiration. Shapes are sculpted by hand and then painted with acrylic paints. Charms are edged in gold to add detail and warmth to painted woodland themed charms.

①

FOR THE CHARMS

- Polymer clay in white and small amounts of beige, brown, green, and black
- Needle tool
- Wire for loops
- Two black seed beads for fox eyes
- Orange and red acrylic paint
- Brown acrylic paint or antiquing medium, optional
- Gold bronzing powder
- Brush for powder
- Polymer clay varnish
- Paintbrush

Step 1: Form clay charms by sculpting each into figures. This photo shows the clay parts before assembly and the progression for making each. Before baking, insert a twisted wire loop into the top of each figure for hanging the charms.

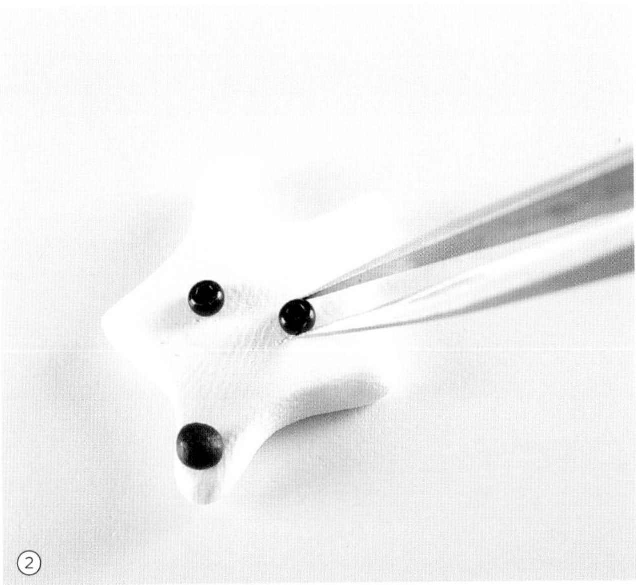

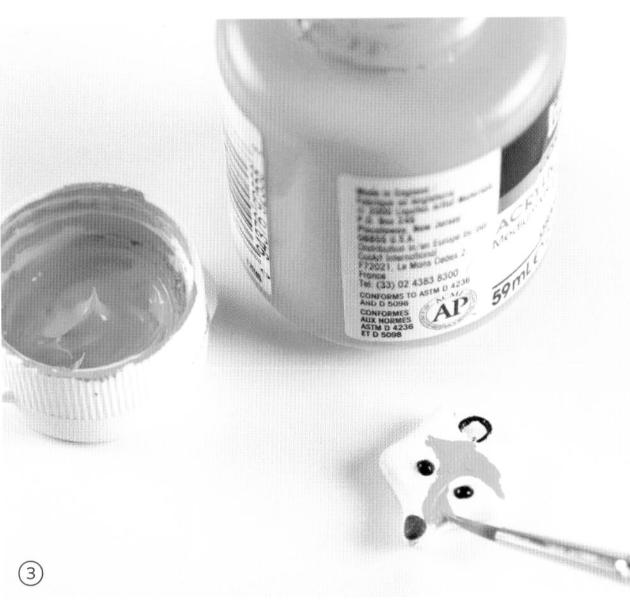

Step 2: To make the fox charm, shape a fox head as shown with white clay. The head is formed by making a five-point star shape, with one of the points longer for the nose. Push small seed beads into the clay for the eyes. Roll a small ball of black clay and press onto the longer point for the nose.

Step 3: Bake the fox charm according to the manufacturer's instructions and allow to cool. Use light orange acrylic paint to add details resembling the markings of a red fox.

Step 4: Form the other charms as shown in step 1. Shape the mushroom and then press dots of clay onto the mushroom cap. Use a knife or needle tool to score the underside of the cap with gills. Bake according to the manufacturer's instructions and allow to cool. Paint the cap with red acrylic paint. Make the leaf charm using a clay mold or form one by hand. Form the dogwood flower by assembling four heart shapes into a circle. Press a small ball of green clay into the center and add texture with a needle tool. Form the acorn by rolling a small ball of light tan clay into a ball. Pinch the ball to form a point. Add a cap by pressing a small flat circle of brown clay onto the top. Texture the surface of the cap with a needle tool.

Step 5: Bake all charms according to the manufacturer's instructions before adding painted details. Add gold powder around the edges of the charms using polymer clay varnish as an adhesive. Paint the varnish around the edges of the baked charms. Add the powder by tapping the powder onto the wet varnish or applying it with a soft brush. After the varnish dries, add another layer of varnish to seal the powder in place.

FOR THE BRACELET

- 1 yard (1 m) brown embroidery floss
- 1 yard (1 m) green embroidery floss
- 1 yard (1 m) yellow embroidery floss
- 8 inch (20.5 cm) curb chain
- Accent beads
- Jump rings
- Head pins
- Wire cutters
- Pliers

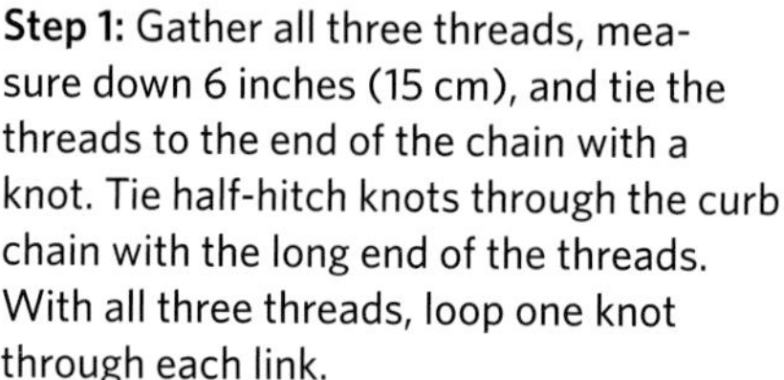

Step 1: Gather all three threads, measure down 6 inches (15 cm), and tie the threads to the end of the chain with a knot. Tie half-hitch knots through the curb chain with the long end of the threads. With all three threads, loop one knot through each link.

Step 2: When the knots are complete, fasten the end of the threads to the last link with an overhand knot. Clip off the excess thread, leaving a short length at each end. Knot small beads on the ends of the threads. Using jump rings, attach the charms to the bracelet. Attach small beads along the thread with head pins. Add a bead to each wire end and form the wire into a loop. Attach to the thread and wrap the wire at the base of the loop, clipping off any excess wire.

①

②

Enchanted Garden

Sculpt or mold charm shapes inspired by nature. The bee in this project is made using a combination of simple clay shapes that are melded together. Rhinestones were imbedded in a few of the charms for added bling. This bracelet utilizes dark brown paint or antiquing medium to emphasize the details of the charms.

FOR THE CHARMS

- Polymer clay in small amounts: pink, green, white, black, yellow, and orange
- Rhinestone chain
- Rhinestones for bee and flower
- Plastic coated wire for loops
- Purchased flower and leaf molds, optional
- Needle tool
- Craft knife
- Cornstarch or baby powder for mold
- Acrylic paint or antiquing medium
- Polymer clay varnish
- Paintbrush

FOR THE BRACELET

- Small piece of curb chain for charms
- 2 yards (1.8 m) of embroidery floss in six colors: black, yellow, orange, light pink, coral, and white, each cut into 1 yard (1 m)-lengths
- Jump rings
- Scissors
- Round nose pliers

MAKING THE CHARMS

Step 1: Form clay charms by sculpting each into figures. This photo shows the clay parts before assembly and the progression for making each. Insert a twisted wire loop for hanging the charms into the top of each before baking. Purchased molds were used to form the flowers and leaves. They can also be sculpted freehand. Score lines or veins into the pieces to add texture. Press rhinestones into the center of the flowers if desired. The rose bud consists of three petal shapes and a star shape for the sepal. Roll one petal for the center and overlap the petals around the center. Pinch the green sepal at the base of the rose bud before adding the wire loop. Assemble the bee using the clay shapes shown. Press the parts together to adhere. Press small pieces of rhinestone chain into the body of the bee to form stripes. Press a rhinestone under the head of the bee and add score lines to the wings.

Step 2: If you are using a purchased clay mold for the flowers, dust the mold with cornstarch or baby powder to prevent the clay from sticking. To form the center of the flower, press a small ball of orange clay into the middle of the mold. Press yellow clay into the mold over the orange center to create the flower.

Step 3: Press or roll the back of the clay and remove the flower from the mold. Trim off the excess clay around the flower. Embed loops in all of the charms and then bake according to the manufacturer's instructions. When cool, rub acrylic paint or antiquing medium into the recessed areas of the texture. Seal with a layer of matte or gloss varnish.

KNOTTING THE BRACELET

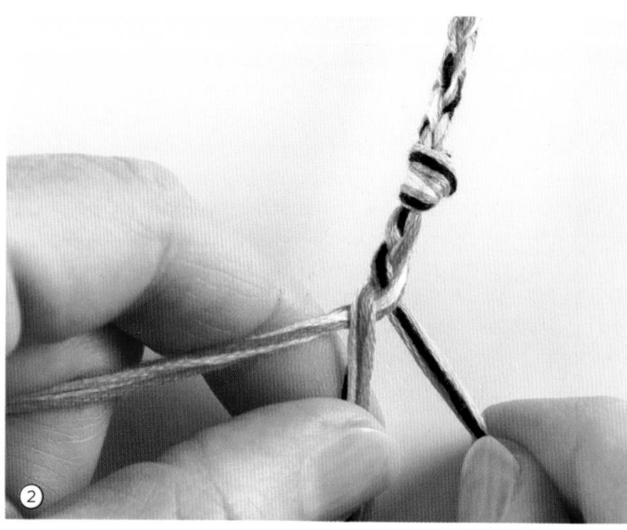

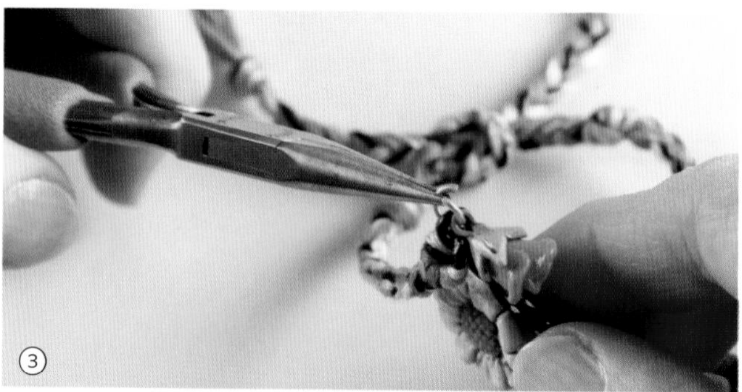

Step 1: Gather six threads, each cut to a length of 1 yard (1 m). Double the threads and attach to the end of the chain with a lark's head loop as shown on page 39. Divide the threads into four sections and braid the bracelet pattern with a four-strand braid. Stop braiding when the braid with chain attached is long enough to wrap halfway around your wrist. Repeat the pattern on the other side of the bracelet.

Step 2: Tie an overhand knot on each side to make ties for the bracelet by dividing the threads into three sections and braiding with a three-strand braid to finish. Tie with an overhand knot to secure the ends. Clip off the excess thread.

Step 3: Attach the charms to the bracelet with jump rings. See page 43 for how to open and shut jump rings with pliers.

Island Paradise

Bright and whimsical, this is the perfect bracelet to wear on a tropical cruise. The popular Plumeria flower is featured in this design. All of the charms on this bracelet were highlighted with pigment powders that contain mica powder, which adds a shimmer to the color. Powders applied to baked clay are rubbed onto the surface and can be blended by layering. To retain the shimmery look, seal the powders with polymer clay varnish.

FOR THE CHARMS

- Polymer clay in small amounts of white, yellow, orange, and green
- Teardrop shaped clay cutters
- Flower cutters (available through cake decorator suppliers)
- Clay sculpting tool
- Needle tool
- Wire for loops
- Rhinestone for center of flowers, optional
- Pigment powders in pink and yellow
- Three paintbrushes
- Red, yellow, and brown acrylic paint
- Polymer clay varnish

MAKING THE CHARMS

Step 1: Form clay charms by sculpting each into floral forms. This photo shows the clay parts before assembly and the progression for making each. Insert a twisted wire loop for hanging the charms into the top of each before baking. Form flower and leaf charms by rolling sheets of clay and then cutting shapes with teardrop shaped clay cutters or flower shapes made for cake decorating. Cut green teardrop shapes for the leaves. Score veins with a knife or needle tool in the leaf. Form flower petals by cutting teardrop shapes and then sculpting them to look more realistic. Some flowers are assembled with the point of the teardrop facing towards the center and others facing out. Make centers with small balls of clay. Press the clay petals together well. Add rhinestones if desired for sparkle.

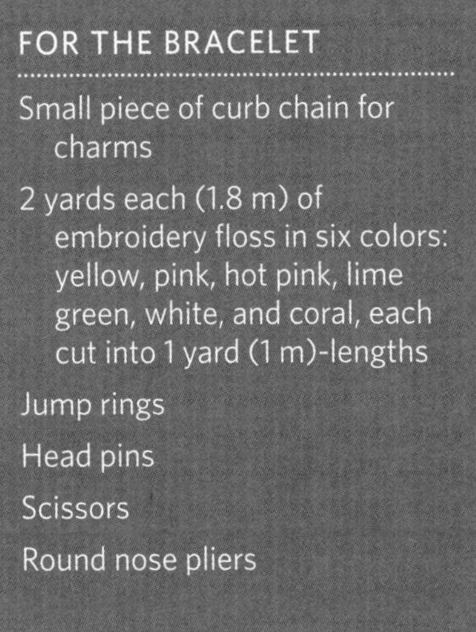

FOR THE BRACELET

- Small piece of curb chain for charms
- 2 yards each (1.8 m) of embroidery floss in six colors: yellow, pink, hot pink, lime green, white, and coral, each cut into 1 yard (1 m)-lengths
- Jump rings
- Head pins
- Scissors
- Round nose pliers

②

HINT *After baking the flowers, you can reinforce the flower by pressing a ball of clay in the center of the petals on the back. Flatten the clay and re-bake. This will help to keep the fragile petals from breaking during wear and tear.*

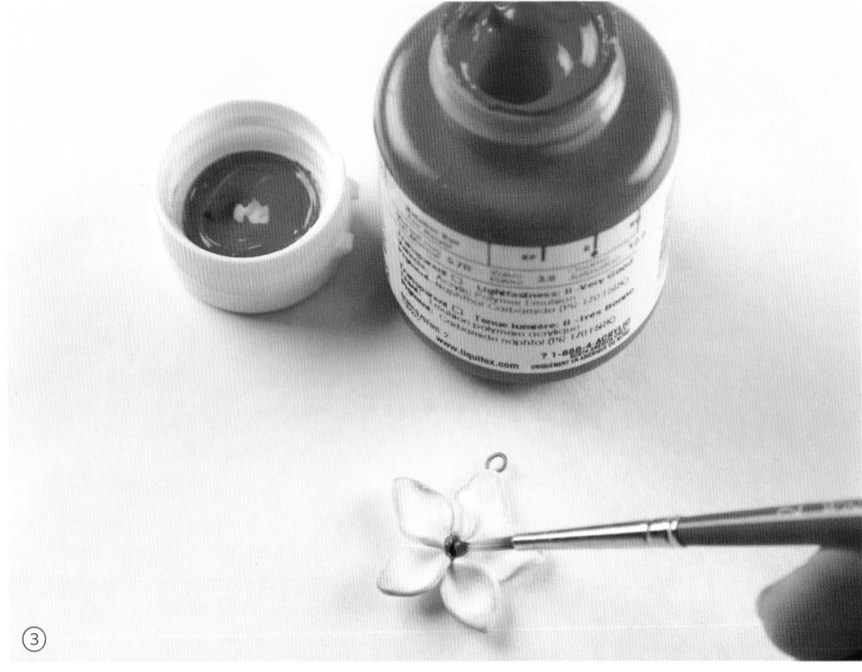

③

KNOTTING THE BRACELET

To string the bracelet, follow the same instructions for the Enchanted Garden bracelet on page 96, using a chain and thread. The thread colors used for this bracelet are yellow, pink, hot pink, lime green, white, and coral. Attach accent beads to the chain with head pins.

Step 2: To make the white Plumeria flower, roll out a sheet of white clay. Cut five petal shapes with a teardrop shaped cutter. Pinch to elongate and to create a crease at the rounded end. Arrange the petals in a circle with the points facing out. Press the petals together in the center with a clay sculpting tool. Pierce a hole in the center of the flower with a needle tool. Insert a wire loop and bake the flower. Brush pink pigment powder around the edges of the petals. Apply yellow pigment powder to the center of the flower. Use a small cloth or your fingers to buff the pigment onto the surface of the clay.

Step 3: Add details to the flowers and leaves with acrylic paint. Paint the center of the Plumeria with a cool red color. Paint leaf veins with yellow or brown paint. When the paint dries, seal the powder with matte varnish.

Beachy Keen

Natural sea glass is formed when glass shards are rolled and tumbled in the ocean over many years. Salt water and persistent tumbling produce translucent glass pieces with rounded corners and a frosted appearance. Tinted translucent polymer clay is the perfect medium to use for making faux sea glass. You can shape the clay to form beads and natural shapes with large holes, which are perfect for stringing.

FOR THE BEADS

- Translucent polymer clay, such as Pardo
- Blue and green alcohol inks
- Rubber gloves
- Needle tool
- Bead wire

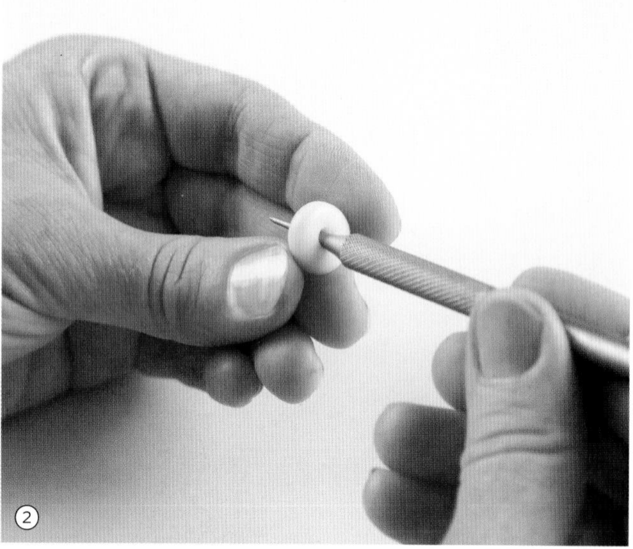

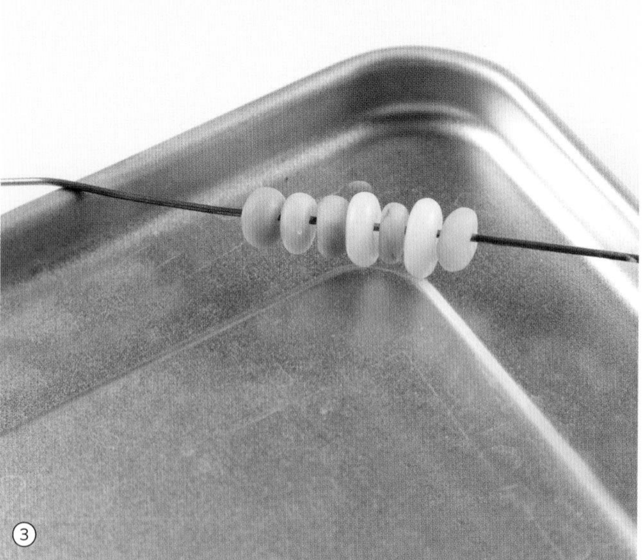

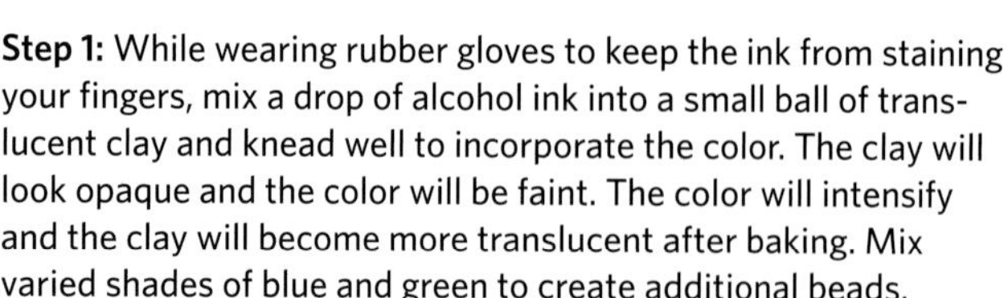

Step 1: While wearing rubber gloves to keep the ink from staining your fingers, mix a drop of alcohol ink into a small ball of translucent clay and knead well to incorporate the color. The clay will look opaque and the color will be faint. The color will intensify and the clay will become more translucent after baking. Mix varied shades of blue and green to create additional beads.

Step 2: Form the beads into flattened round shapes and pierce a hole through the beads prior to baking.

Step 3: Bake the beads flat on a baking sheet lined with paper or suspended on a wire. Bake according to the required temperature and time appropriate for the clay you are using.

FOR THE BRACELET

Blue embroidery floss, 1 length 60 inches (152.5 cm) long

Yellow embroidery floss, 1 length 60 inches (152.5 cm) long

White embroidery floss, 1 length 60 inches (152.5 cm) long

Scissors

Fine wire for stringing

Step 1: Cut three threads each 60 inches (152.5 cm) long in blue, yellow, and white. Gather them together and measure down about 28 inches (71 cm) to form a loop for the bracelet closure. To make the loop, use one of the threads (blue in this case) to tie a series of lark's head knots over the other two threads, which will serve as the core. Tie enough knots to make a small loop. Form the loop and bring all thread ends straight down to begin knotting the bracelet. See page 39 for the lark's head loop instructions. You will now have six threads, two of each color. Bring two threads to the center to serve as the core and keep two threads to each side. Tie a series of square knots with the outside threads as shown.

Step 2: After tying 2 to 2½ inches (5 to 6.5 cm) of knots, tie an overhand knot. Use a fine wire to thread the sea glass beads over all of the cords at the center of the bracelet. Finish with another overhand knot to secure the beads. Resume tying square knots to complete the other side of the bracelet. When the bracelet is the desired length, finish by separating the threads into two sections, braiding each with a three-strand braid pattern for about 2½ to 3 inches (6.5 cm to 7.5 cm) to serve as the ties for fastening the bracelet. Add a clay bead to the end of each braid with an overhand knot to finish.

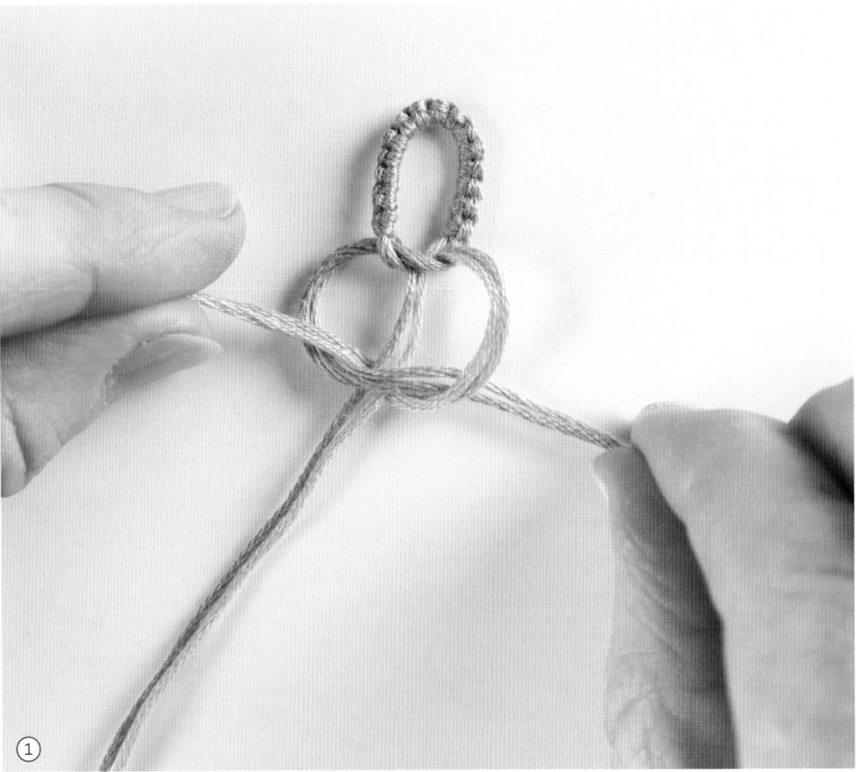

①

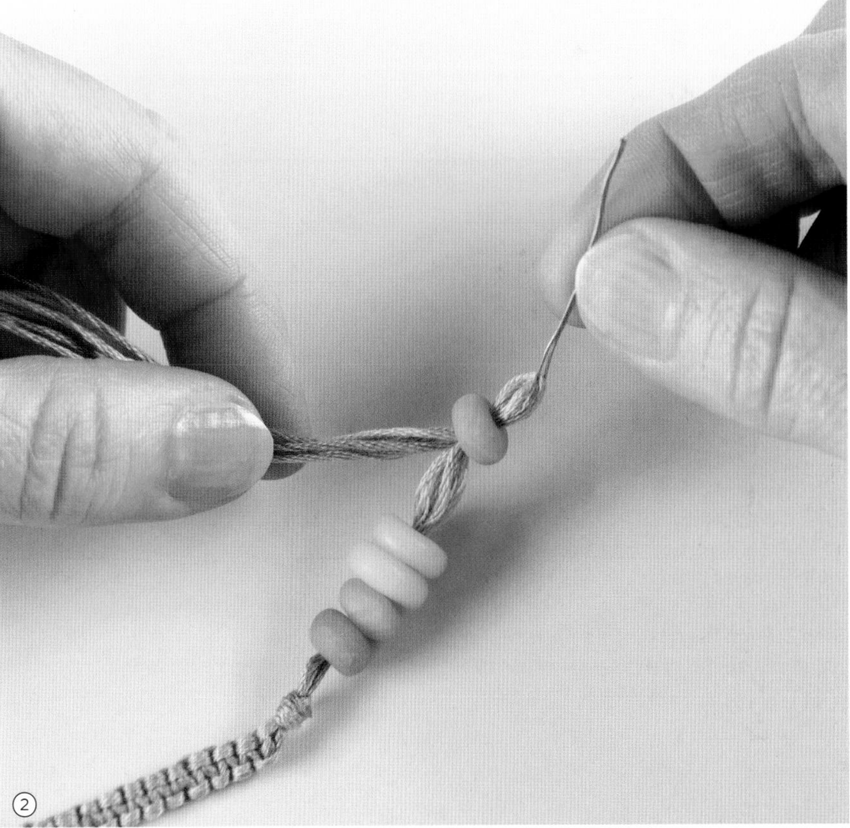

②

Silver Threads

Transform lace into a silvery jewelry piece by molding it with clay. Crocheted lace is especially good to use because it produces deep textures for the mold, which is then transferred to the final clay piece. Metallic paints transform the clay, making it look like metal. Metallic threads and chain add shimmer and the texture to coordinate with the metal clay lace.

MAKING THE CHARM

FOR THE CHARM

- Two-part silicone mold putty
- Heavy crocheted lace to mold
- Silver polymer clay
- Ceramic mug (curved baking form)
- Silver acrylic paint
- Silver metallic powder
- Three paintbrushes
- Polymer clay varnish
- Antiquing medium
- Knife
- Roller

①

②

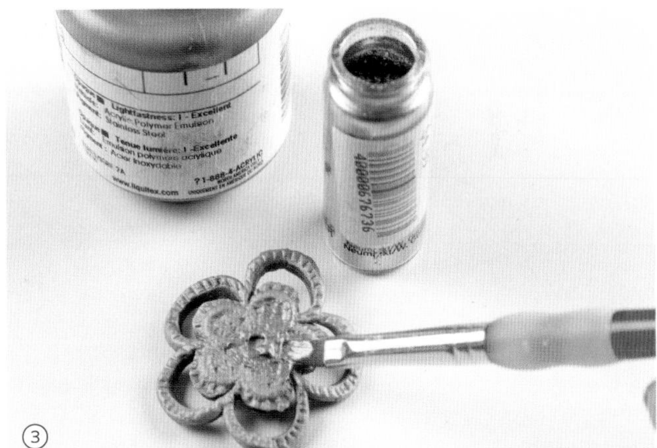

③

Step 1: Mix the two-part silicone mold putty to make a lace pattern mold. Press a piece of real lace into the mixed putty. Let it cure and remove the lace.

Step 2: After the mold cures, press silver polymer clay into the mold, rolling it smooth over the back of the clay to flatten. Remove the clay from the mold and trim the background and negative areas away from the clay lace using a knife. Refine or repair details as needed with sculpting tools. Drape the clay lace over an oven-safe ceramic mug to maintain a soft curve form while baking. Bake the piece according to the directions on page 20.

Step 3: After cooling, paint the clay surface with a layer of metallic silver acrylic paint. Apply metallic powder with a small brush while the paint is still tacky for more brilliance. After the piece is dry, seal the surface with a clear polymer clay varnish and allow to dry. You can antique the surface by rubbing it with antiquing medium. Wipe off the excess using a barely damp paper towel.

FOR THE BRACELET

- 16 feet (5 m) silver metallic cord, cut into four pieces, each measuring 4 feet (1.2 m) long
- Two pieces of chain
- Lobster claw clasp
- One small jump ring
- Two jump rings
- Pliers
- Two-part epoxy resin and toothpick
- Waxed paper

①

②

③

Step 1: The bracelet is formed by tying a series of lark's head knots along both sides of a chain using a metallic cord. Start by folding one of the cords with 12 inches (30.5 cm) on one end and 36 inches (91.5 cm) on the other. Keep the 36 inches (91.5 cm) long cord to the inside and attach with a lark's head knot to the clay lace. This cord will be used to work down the right side of the chain. Loop the long end of the cord through the end of a piece of chain and tie the first half of a lark's head knot.

Step 2: Tie the second half of the knot without passing it through the chain. Continue tying lark's head knots down the chain, passing the cord under and through each link before tying the next knot.

Step 3: Fold another cord to work down the left side of the chain. Loop the cord through the clay lace, attaching with a lark's head knot. Leave the outside cord 12 inches (30.5 cm) long. Loop the long end of the cord through the left side of the chain with the first half of a lark's head knot. Continue down the left side of the chain with a series of lark's head knots as you did on the right side.

④

Step 4: Repeat the lark's head knots with the remaining cords and chain to complete the other side of the bracelet. Finish off by knotting the cords on the back side of the chain with square knots. Apply epoxy resin to secure the knots and clip off the ends of the cord. Remove excess chain if needed. Use pliers to attach a small jump ring with lobster claw clasp to one side. Attach a large jump ring to the other end of the chain for the clasp.

Beyond the Fringe

Small pieces of cut chain add movement and sparkle to a simple braided design using metallic cords and threads. Use random lengths and group the chain sections using two or more at a time, sewing them along the bracelet for an icicle effect. The final bracelet is dripping with silver for an elegant feel on your wrist.

FOR THE CHARM

- Two-part silicone mold putty
- Heavy crocheted lace to mold
- Silver polymer clay
- Silver acrylic paint
- Silver metallic powder
- Two small wires (for loops to embed in lace centerpiece)
- Ceramic mug (curved baking form)
- Antiquing medium
- Knife
- Roller
- Two-part epoxy resin and toothpick

FOR THE BRACELET

- 4 yards (3.7 m) silver cords or threads, cut into 4 pieces 1 yard (1 m) long
- Two pieces of chain to braid with cords, each cut 10 inches (25.5 cm) long
- Four small jump rings
- Fine chain for fringe
- Needle
- Clear microfilament thread
- Large jump ring
- Lobster claw clasp
- Wire cutters
- Pliers

MAKING THE CHARM

Step 1: Follow the instructions from the Silver Threads project, steps 1 through 3 on page 103, to make a clay centerpiece for the bracelet.

Step 2: Embed two wire loops in the sides of the clay prior to baking. These can be secured with epoxy resin after baking.

KNOTTING THE BRACELET

Step 1: Double two silver cords and pass the folded ends through one of the wire loops on the centerpiece. Bring the cord tail ends through the cord loops to form a lark's head with each cord. Attach the other two cords to the other side in the same manner. Use pliers to attach a piece of chain to each side of the centerpiece using a small jump ring to affix the chain to the wire loops next to the cords. Braid the threads along with the chain using a 3-strand braid pattern as shown on page 25, repeating on both sides until the bracelet fits. Hold the chain alongside of one of the cords or threads as you braid. Attach a large jump ring to the end of one finished braid and a lobster claw to the other end using an overhand knot to secure both. Leave just a small tail of cord at the end of the bracelet and clip off the excess cord and chain.

Step 2: Divide a fine chain by cutting it into small pieces with wire cutters. Thread a needle with clear microfilament thread and stitch sections of chain along the braid to create fringe made of chain. Knot the monofilament when finished.

Torch Song

Lampworking is the art of creating glass beads by melting glass with a torch and forming the molten glass around a mandrel. To mimic lampwork beads with polymer clay, embed glass dots into the clay and coat with liquid polymer clay. The liquid polymer clay provides a glasslike coating to the clay when heated. Small dichroic glass dots can be purchased from glass blowing and stained glass supply companies.

FOR THE BEADS

- Polymer clay in various colors to form round beads
- Small dichroic glass dots
- Liquid polymer clay
- Paintbrush
- Wire for baking beads
- Embossing heat tool

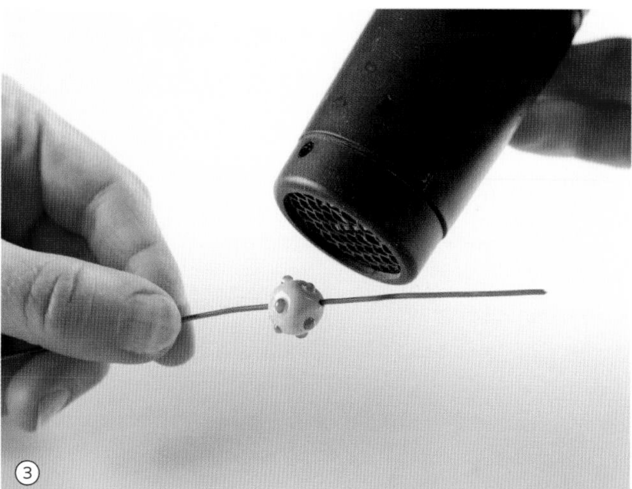

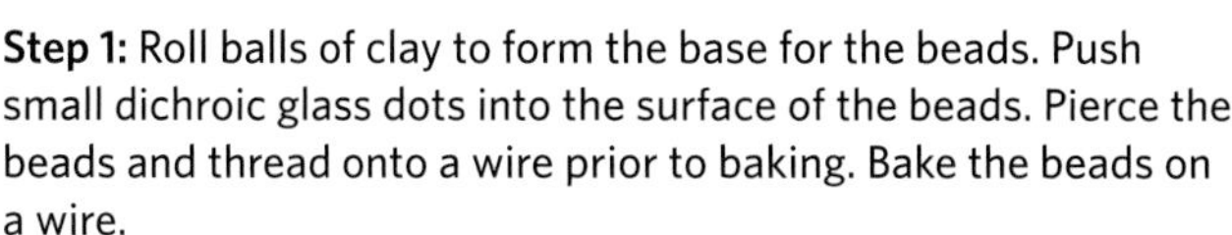

Step 1: Roll balls of clay to form the base for the beads. Push small dichroic glass dots into the surface of the beads. Pierce the beads and thread onto a wire prior to baking. Bake the beads on a wire.

Step 2: Suspend a single bead on a wire to hold it while you coat the bead with liquid polymer. Paint a layer of liquid polymer to surround the bead.

Step 3: Heat the surface of the bead with an embossing heat tool, rotating the bead on the wire as you apply heat to prevent the liquid from dripping off and to prevent burning. Stop heating when the liquid polymer turns clear. After the bead is cool, twist it off the wire.

FOR THE BRACELET

2 yards (1.8 m) bead cord, cut one cord 30 inches, (76 cm) and the other 42 inches (106.5 cm)

E beads

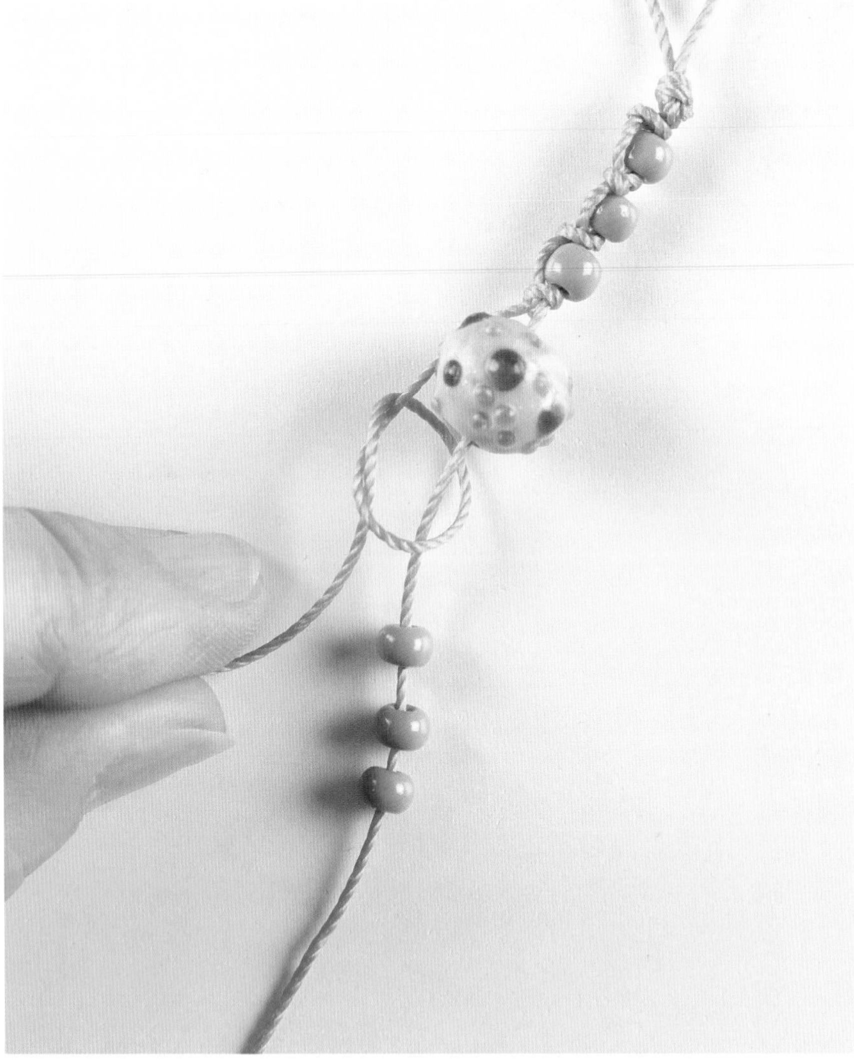

Gather both cords and tie an overhand knot about 10 inches (25.5 cm) from the ends of the cords to begin. Pull the shorter cord straight down to serve as the core to which the beads will be added. Tie an overhand knot using the long cord, tying it over the core. Add a glass E bead to the core and slide it up close to the knot. Tie another overhand knot with the long cord, securing the knot under the E bead. Continue this pattern to form the bracelet. Add clay beads as you go, along with other beads as desired to create a design. When the bracelet fits your wrist, tie an overhand knot using both cords. Bring the ends of the cords together and use a small piece of cord to tie over them with a square knot closure as shown on page 41. Tie E beads to the ends of the cords, securing them with overhand knots.

Hello Sunshine

Caneworking is a popular technique used to produce intricate designs with polymer clay. This technique is borrowed from glass blowing, using long rods of clay that are assembled, reduced, and then cut into small sections. Intricate patterns are found within these sections. For clean, neat-looking patterns, use contrasting colors of polymer clay and assemble the shapes tightly together. The pattern will become smaller as you roll the cane into a thinner rod. For best results, use a firm brand of polymer clay rather than a soft version.

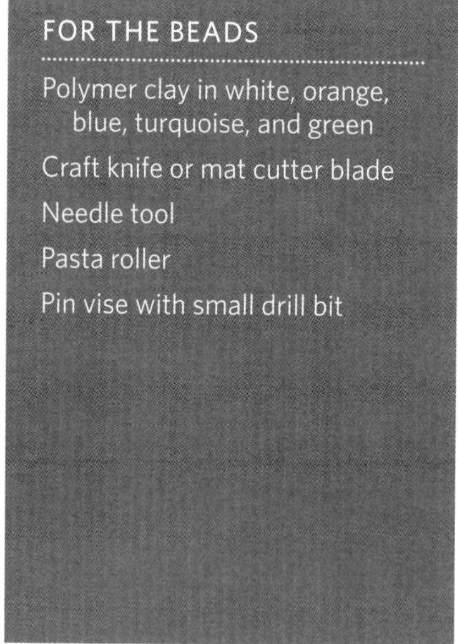

FOR THE BEADS

- Polymer clay in white, orange, blue, turquoise, and green
- Craft knife or mat cutter blade
- Needle tool
- Pasta roller
- Pin vise with small drill bit

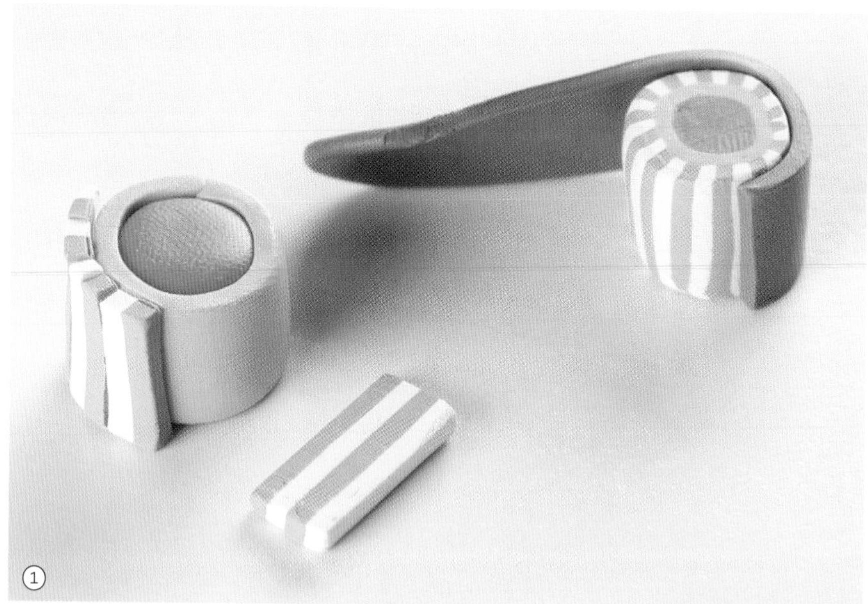

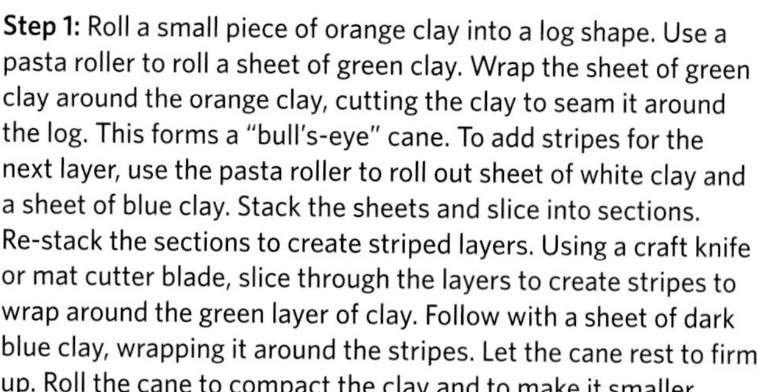

Step 1: Roll a small piece of orange clay into a log shape. Use a pasta roller to roll a sheet of green clay. Wrap the sheet of green clay around the orange clay, cutting the clay to seam it around the log. This forms a "bull's-eye" cane. To add stripes for the next layer, use the pasta roller to roll out sheet of white clay and a sheet of blue clay. Stack the sheets and slice into sections. Re-stack the sections to create striped layers. Using a craft knife or mat cutter blade, slice through the layers to create stripes to wrap around the green layer of clay. Follow with a sheet of dark blue clay, wrapping it around the stripes. Let the cane rest to firm up. Roll the cane to compact the clay and to make it smaller.

Step 2: Roll out a thick sheet of blue and a sheet of yellow green clay, using the thickest setting on the pasta roller. Fold each sheet in half to double the thickness of the clays. Cut each thick slab of clay into a rectangle shape. Using a craft knife or mat cutter blade, cut through the slab at a 45-degree angle, first one way and then the other, to cut triangle-shaped strips from both slabs of clay. Arrange them by alternating the blue and yellow-green clays strips. Assemble enough to wrap around the cane.

Step 3: After wrapping the triangle strips around the cane, wrap the outside of the cane with a sheet of the same blue color that was used for the strips. Finish by wrapping the cane with a sheet of orange clay. Cut the clay ends of the wrapped clay to seam the ends. Let the cane rest for a few hours until firm.

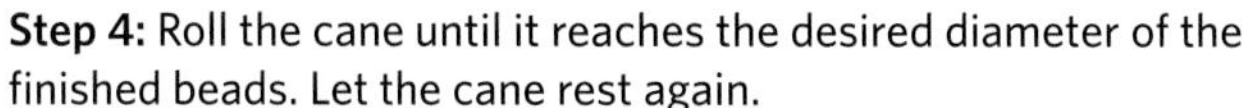

Step 4: Roll the cane until it reaches the desired diameter of the finished beads. Let the cane rest again.

Step 5: To make the beads, use a craft knife or mat cutter blade to slice beads from the cane. Pierce a hole through the side of each bead before baking. The hole can be enlarged after baking with a pin vise and small drill bit. Bake the beads. Make additional beads using the same cane elements but varying the color and the order of assembly: bull's-eye, stripes, and triangle wedges wrapped with sheets of clay between each addition.

Step 6: After baking the beads, use a pin vise with a small drill bit to enlarge the holes for stringing, if necessary.

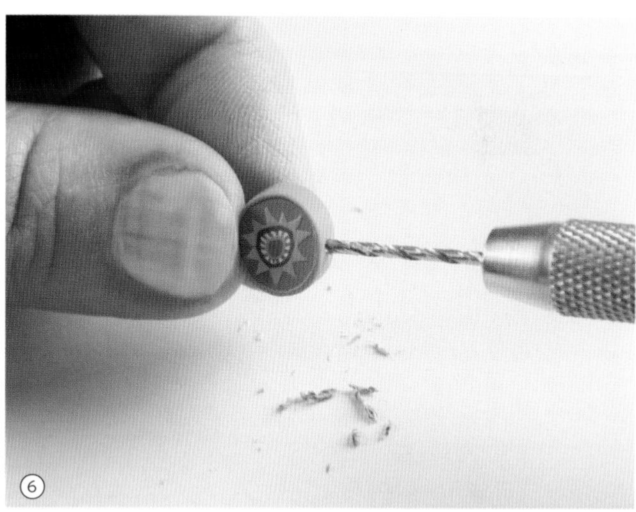

KNOTTING THE BRACELET

FOR THE BRACELET

- 4 yards (3.7 m) nylon beading cord, cut into 4 sections of 1 yard (1 m) each
- Small accent beads to alternate with clay beads, optional

Gather four cords measuring 1 yard (1 m) each to begin knotting the bracelet. Measure down about 10 inches (25.5 cm) and tie an overhand knot with all of the cords. Tie a series of square knots to form the pattern. Thread caned beads alternated with accent beads onto the core cords with square knots inbetween. Bring the tying cords down along the sides of each bead as it is added. Tie a few square knots between each bead. To finish the bracelet, tie all cords with an overhand knot and add small beads to the cord ends to tie. Alternatively, you can add a square knot slide as a closure as shown on page 41.

Flower Child

Flower canes are made using leftover cane slices from bull's-eye or sunburst designs. Any round cane will do. Simply assemble round canes around a coordinating center to form petals and you have an instant flower design. Flower beads look great for a casual macramé bracelet design. Use hemp cord instead of nylon for a traditional macramé bracelet look.

FOR THE BEADS

- Leftover bull's-eye and sunburst canes
- White polymer clay
- Solid color of polymer clay (any color)
- Craft knife or mat cutter blade
- Needle tool

FOR THE BRACELET

- 4 yards (3.7 m) nylon beading cord, cut into 4 sections measuring 1 yard (1 m) each
- Small accent beads to alternate with clay beads, optional

MAKING THE BEADS

Step 1: To make a flower cane, you will need five sections cut from a round cane for petals with one section cut from a bull's-eye cane for the flower center. Shape the five canes to be used for the petals into long teardrop shapes and slice off the pointed end of each shape. Assemble them around the bull's-eye cane to make a flower. Fill in the negative areas between the petals with white or another solid color as shown. Wrap the cane components with a strip of clay that matches the background color (white in this case).

Step 2: Let the cane rest until firm. Roll the cane on its side to lengthen and reduce the size. Wrap the cane again with a solid color of clay. Rest the cane and then roll to compact the clay. Slice off sections to make beads and then pierce holes in the cane as directed for the Hello Sunshine project before baking. Bake the beads.

KNOTTING THE BRACELET

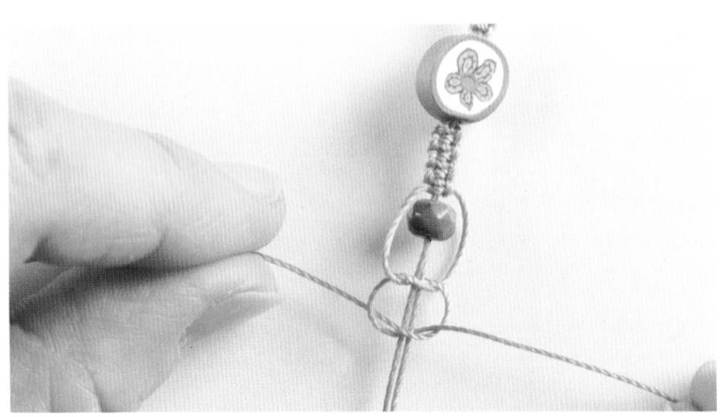

String the beads with square knots following the steps for the Hello Sunshine project, using your choice of cord color and beads.

True Blue

Filigree-type bead caps work well to encase polymer clay because the filigree has holes that grip the clay. Decorate the sides of the beads with rhinestone chain, small spacer beads, or single stones. This design features a fold-over clasp to create a multistrand bracelet. Alternatively, you could make an extra-long single strand for a multiple wrap style.

FOR THE BEADS

- Blue polymer clay (or mix desired color—royal blue color was mixed for these beads)
- Filigree bead cap findings
- Small ball chain, rhinestone chain, or small metal spacer beads to embed and decorate beads
- Needle for piercing holes
- Pin vise with small drill bit
- Two-part epoxy resin and toothpick
- Waxed paper

HINT *If any of the elements come off of the bead after baking, you can glue them in place with two-part epoxy resin.*

Step 1: Mix the desired clay color and form small balls of clay for the beads. Press a bead cap on each end of each bead. Press a chain or small rhinestone beads to decorate the exposed clay around the bead.

Step 2: Pass a needle through the bead caps and formed clay bead to make sure the holes align for stringing. If needed, you can enlarge the holes after baking with a pin vise with small drill bit. Bake the beads.

①

②

FOR THE BRACELET

- 7½ yards (7 m) blue nylon cord, cut into three pieces measuring 90 inches (228.6 cm) each
- Rhinestone beads and spacer beads
- Two flat crimp over clasps
- Jump rings and lobster claw for closure
- White glue
- Pliers

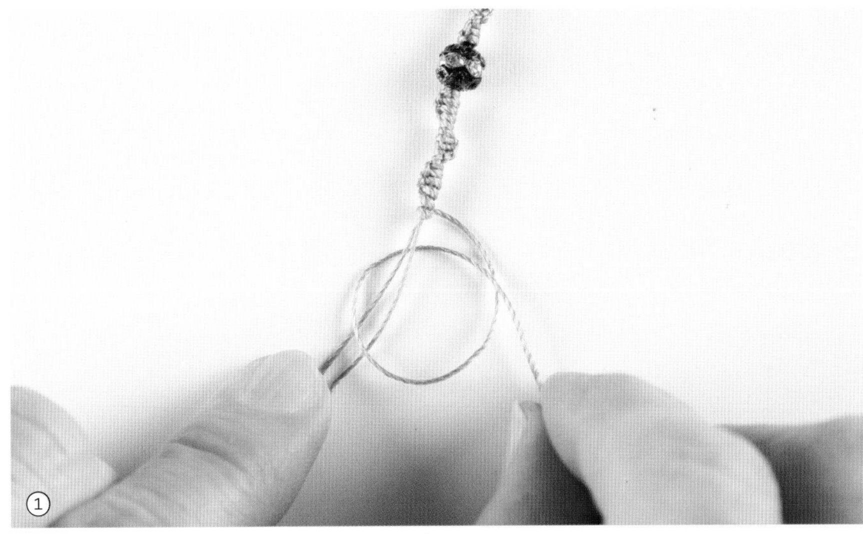

Step 1: To make the bracelet, three separate strands are tied with spiral half hitch knots and then crimped together at each end of the bracelet with a fold over crimp clasp. Cut each 90-inch (228.6 cm) cord into two pieces, one 60 inches (152.5 cm) in length, and the other 30 inches (76 cm). Begin with one of the 30-inch (76 cm) lengths of cords. Double the cord and attach a fine wire to the center (you will have two cord ends measuring 15 inches [38 cm] long coming down from the wire). Bring the end of one of the 60-inch (152.5 cm) lengths even with the ends of the 15-inch (38 cm) lengths. Tie all three cords together with an overhand knot. This knot will be the starting point at the end of the strand. The wire on the doubled 15-inch (38 cm) section will be used to thread beads. The 60-inch (152.5 cm) piece is the longest and will be used to tie spiral knots over the 15-inch (38 cm) lengths, which will serve as the core. Use the 60-inch (152.5 cm) piece to begin tying a series of spiral half hitch knots. Add spacer beads, rhinestone beads, and clay beads along the way, passing all three cords through each bead. It is easiest to pass the long 60-inch (152.5 cm) cord through the bead first and then use the wire to thread the 15-inch (38 cm) lengths through. Knot until a desired length is reached. Make sure you account for the clasp length to obtain a proper fit. Knot the cords with an overhand knot to finish. Repeat the process to make two more strands with the remaining cords.

Step 2: Clip the ends of the cords close to the end knots. Gather the three strands to slip inside the clasp. Apply white glue to the end of each knot to help hold the knots in place inside the fold over clasp before you crimp down. Let the glue dry. This will allow you to pick up the cords and clasp without losing them.

Step 3: Crimp down on the clasp with pliers. Repeat gluing and crimping at the other end of the cords. Use pliers to add a large jump ring to one crimp and then attach a smaller jump ring with a lobster style clasp to the other end.

Sweet Bee

Capture a vintage illustration as the inspiration to make a themed bracelet. Personalize the design by using a photo of a loved one, pet, or a favorite work of art. Any image will work as long as it is a high-resolution image. Reduce the image to fit a bracelet-sized clay cabochon, to which the design will be transferred. Frame the image with beads, thread, or rhinestones. Choices for imagery provide endless possibilities.

FOR THE CHARM

- White clay
- Image Transfer Medium (ITS)
- Transfer paper (ITS paper) with laser printed image (toner)
- Scissors
- Metal filigree
- Polymer clay varnish, matte
- Small seed beads
- Fine monofilament thread
- Two-part epoxy resin and toothpick
- Paintbrush
- Waxed paper
- Nail file (optional)

Step 1: Condition a small ball of white clay. Press it onto a metal filigree jewelry finding, shaping it into an oval shape with a smooth surface. Bake the clay in place on the filigree for 10 minutes. Cool the piece. Copy images onto smooth glossy photo printer paper using a toner laser copier. Cut an image (a bee in this project) to fit the baked clay oval you made in the last step. Make sure the paper edge is even with but not hanging over the edge of the clay. Brush a layer of transfer medium over the clay and press the image face down onto the solution. Press firmly to make sure you have even contact. Bake the piece with the paper adhered at 275°F (135°C, or gas mark 1) for 20 to 25 minutes or until the paper turns to a cream or off-white color. Let it cool.

Step 2: Soak the piece in water until the paper is saturated. Work the paper off with your fingers, starting in the center of the piece. Roll the paper fibers off until smooth, using water to loosen the fibers. The toner will have transferred onto the clay surface. If you make a mistake, you can sand the images off and repeat the transfer process with a new image. Seal the image with a matte polymer clay varnish. If needed, you can use a nail file to refine the edges of the oval after the image is applied.

HINT *If the filigree you are using is large, you may want to bend it with a slight curve to it to fit over the wrist. To curve the piece, bend the filigree over a ceramic mug to shape it prior to adding the clay shape.*

Step 3: To add a beaded bezel around the clay, string seed beads onto fine thread (same as bead color or clear) until you have enough to fit around the shape. Mix a two-part epoxy resin and apply around the edge of the clay with a toothpick. Lay the thread of beads over the epoxy to form the bezel. Let the epoxy cure.

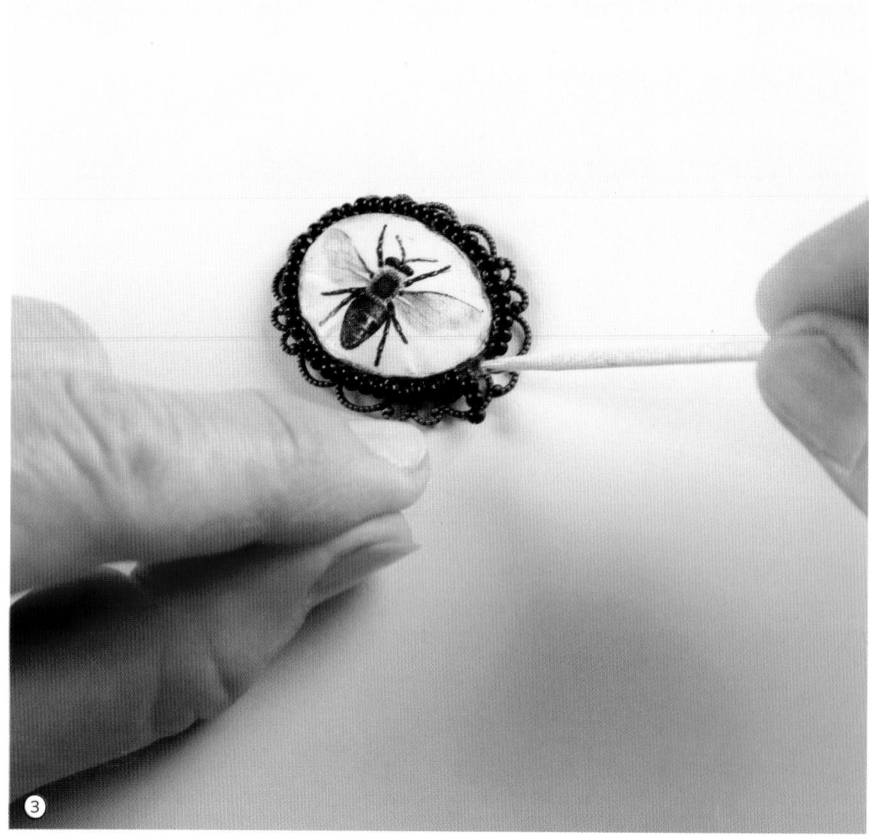

Step 4: Apply the two-part epoxy resin to the back of the filigree, which will keep the clay from separating from the filigree as the bracelet is worn.

FOR THE BRACELET

8 yards (7.3 m) nylon bead cord, cut into eight lengths measuring 1 yard (1 m) each

Small brass beads

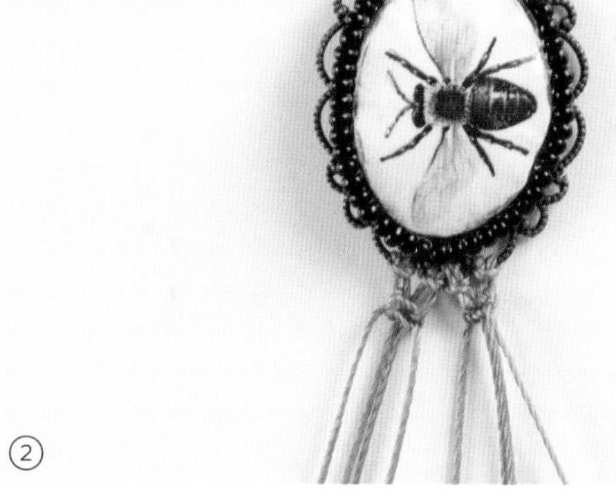

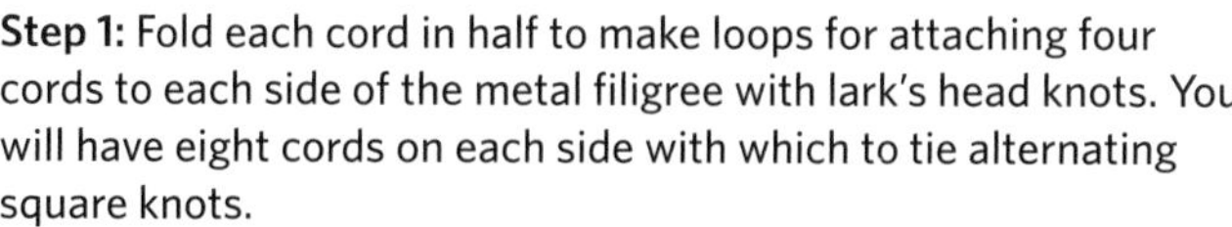

Step 1: Fold each cord in half to make loops for attaching four cords to each side of the metal filigree with lark's head knots. You will have eight cords on each side with which to tie alternating square knots.

Step 2: Start on one side and tie a square knot with the first four cords (1 through 4) and then another with the last four cords (5 through 8) to form two square knots side by side.

Step 3: Tie a single square knot with the middle four cords for the next row—3, 4, 5, 6. Add a bead to cords 2 and 3 and to 6 and 7 in the next row (these will be the core cords used to tie the next square knot).

Step 4: Tie a square knot under each bead (one on each side). Tie a single square knot with the middle four cords for the next row. Repeat the pattern of tying alternating square knots and beads just as you did in the previous steps. When the bracelet is long enough to fit around your wrist, tie with an overhand knot to secure the cords. Braid the cords with a three-strand braid to make ties for each side, finishing with an overhand knot. Clip off the remaining cords.

Botanica

Search old library and textbooks to find detailed botanical illustrations from days gone by. Neutral thread colors add a warm, earthy tone to complement a simple vintage fern illustration. Alternating square knots provide a delicate, lacey pattern for this bracelet.

FOR THE CHARM

- White clay
- Fern image printed on transfer paper (ITS paper)
- Image transfer medium (ITS)
- Metallic thread
- Two-part epoxy resin and toothpick
- Waxed paper

FOR THE BRACELET

- 2 yards (1.8 m) beige embroidery floss, cut into 2 pieces measuring 1 yard (1 m) each
- 2 yards (1.8 m) dark gray embroidery floss, cut into 2 pieces measuring 1 yard (1 m) each
- 2 yards (1.8 m) green embroidery floss, cut into 2 pieces measuring 1 yard (1 m) each

MAKING THE CHARM

Follow the instructions provided for the Sweet Bee bracelet on page 117 to transfer a fern image onto clay. After baking, use two-part epoxy to apply a piece of metallic thread to frame the clay.

KNOTTING THE BRACELET

Step 1: Fold all of the threads in half to make a loop on each thread. Attach one beige thread, one gray thread, and one green thread to each side of the filigree using the loops to form a lark's head attachments with each. Pull the gray middle threads over and place between each of the side threads as shown. One gray thread is placed between the beige threads and one is placed between the green threads. The thread placement of the colors will produce a gradient progression.

Step 2: Tie alternating square knots with the threads to form the bracelet pattern on each side of the bracelet as shown on page 119. This photo shows the first row with a square knot tied on each side.

Step 3: Tie a square knot with the center threads. Repeat the pattern of tying alternating square knots to complete both sides of the bracelet. Finish with an overhand knot on each side. Leave tails of cord for tying.

Social Butterfly

Among vintage illustrations, butterflies are a popular subject. The colorful wings provide inspiration for thread patterns and colors to use for knotting. A two-toned thread design was used for this bracelet. The alternating lark's head knot is fast and easy, making this a perfect project for making gifts or for a fun craft project to make with friends.

FOR THE CHARM

- Round filigree
- White clay
- Butterfly image printed on transfer paper (ITS paper)
- Image transfer medium (ITS)
- Metallic thread
- Two-part epoxy resin and toothpick
- Waxed paper

FOR THE BRACELET

- 2 yards (1.8 m) violet nylon beading cord, cut into 2 pieces measuring 1 yard (1 m) each
- 2 yards (1.8 m) blue nylon beading cord, cut into 2 pieces measuring 1 yard (1 m) each
- Four brass beads

MAKING THE CHARM

Follow the instructions for the Sweet Bee bracelet on page 117 to transfer a butterfly image onto clay. After baking, use the two-part epoxy to apply a piece of metallic thread to frame the clay.

KNOTTING THE BRACELET

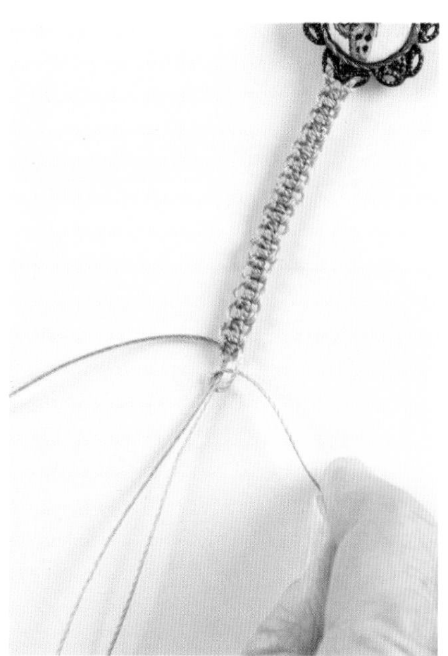

Fold all of the cords in half to make a loop on each cord. Attach one blue cord and one violet cord to each side of the filigree, using the loops to form a lark's head attachment with each. Tie alternating lark's head knots with the cords to form the bracelet pattern on each side of the bracelet. Finish with an overhand knot on each side. Leave tails of cord for tying. Small beads can be knotted to the ends of the cords to finish.

Inner Strength

This bracelet design features a bear fetish—a small shape that Native American Tribes carve from various materials. Fetishes depict animals and icons integral to the culture for ceremonial purposes, and they are carried for good luck or for protection. The bear represents healing and the blue color is associated with curative powers. Add feathers and tassels to embellish this colorful Native American knotted bracelet pattern.

FOR THE CHARM

- Polymer clay
- Sand
- Bear pattern (copy and cut), below
- Sand to texture clay
- Paper
- Scissors
- Craft knife
- Needle tool

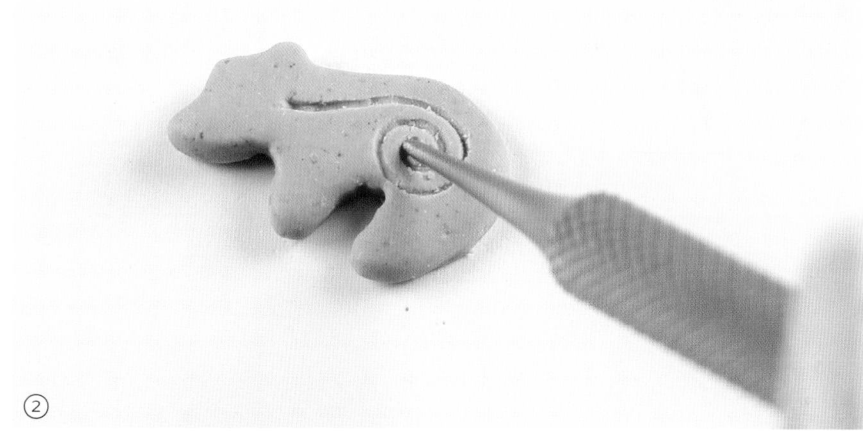

Choose whether you want a small, medium, or large bear charm, and then copy and cut out that template.

Step 1: Mix a shade of turquoise to resemble a muted stone color. Mix a bit of sand into the clay and roll into a thick sheet. Draw a bear shape on paper using the template and cut it out. Lay the paper template on the rolled out clay and use a craft knife to cut around the bear shape.

Step 2: Refine the edges of the bear charm with a sculpting tool and score a design on the surface with a needle tool. Bake the clay shape.

KNOTTING THE BRACELET

FOR THE BRACELET

- Five colors embroidery floss thread, 2 yards (1.8 m) of each color
- Cord for wrapping beads
- Small silver beads to embellish bear
- Scissors
- Card for tassel
- Feather
- White glue

① 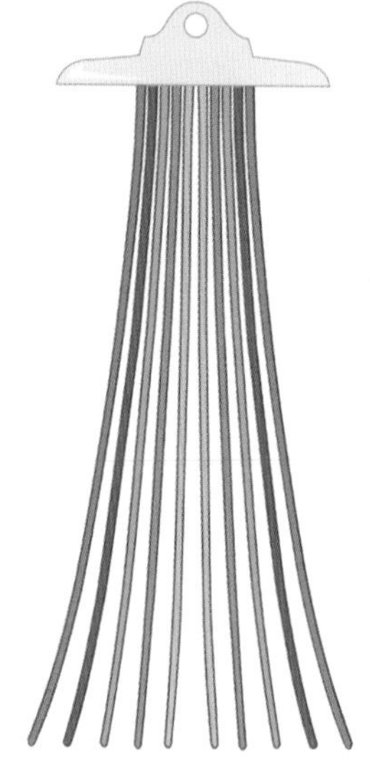

② 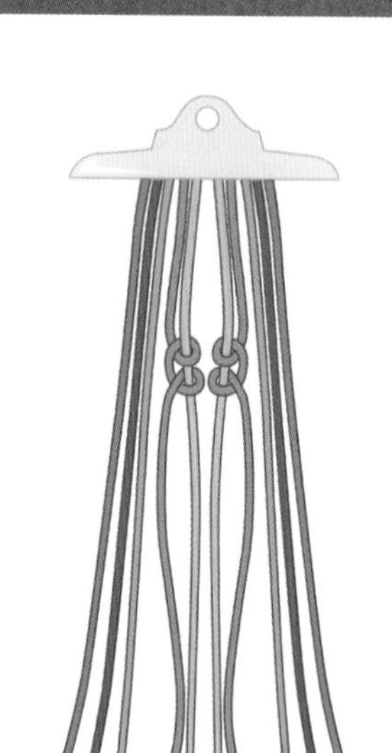

③ 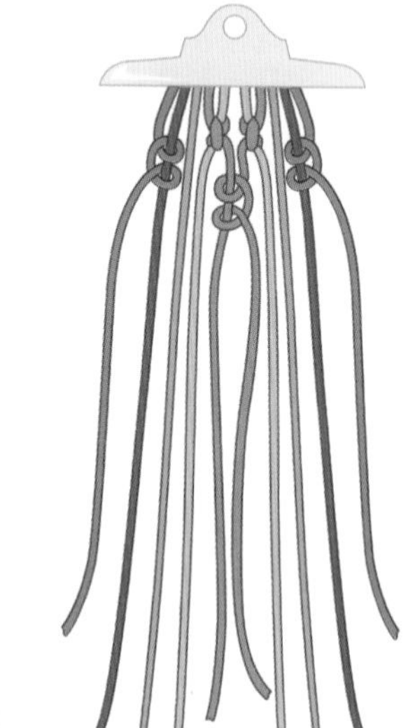

④ 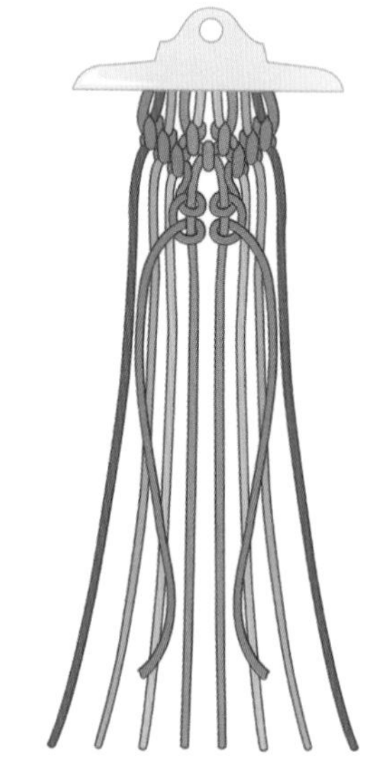

⑤ 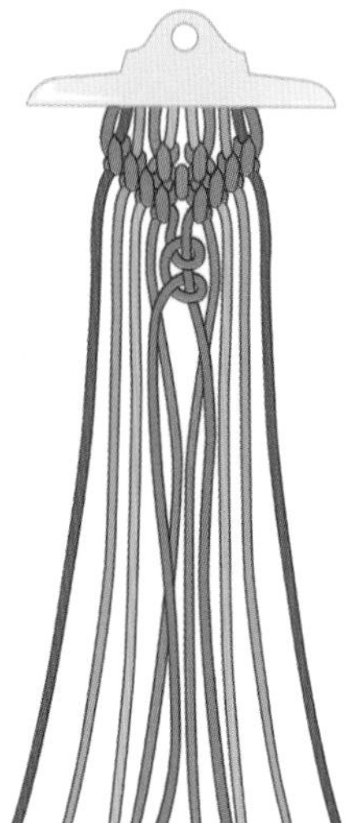

⑥ 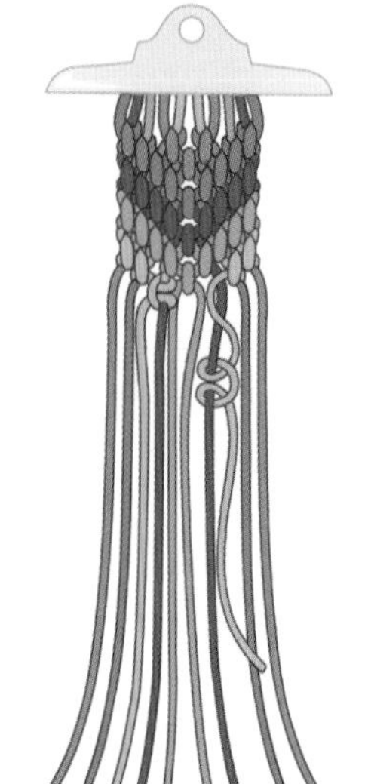

⑦ 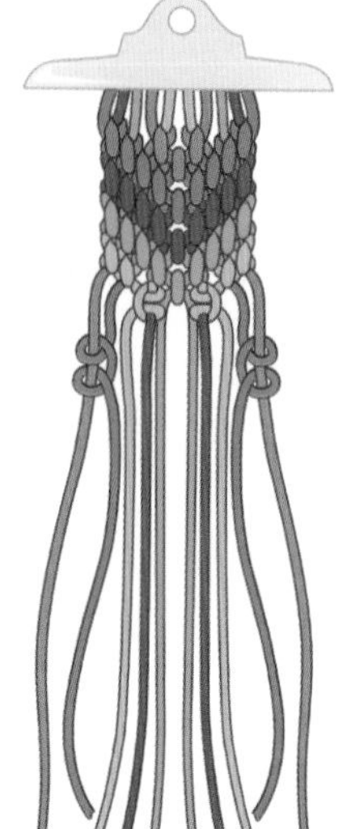

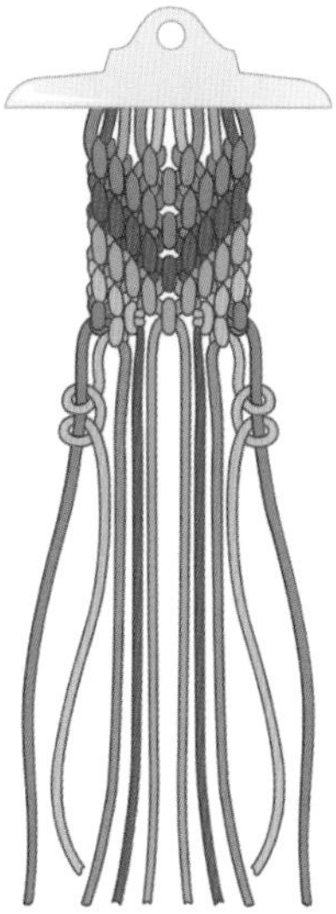

8

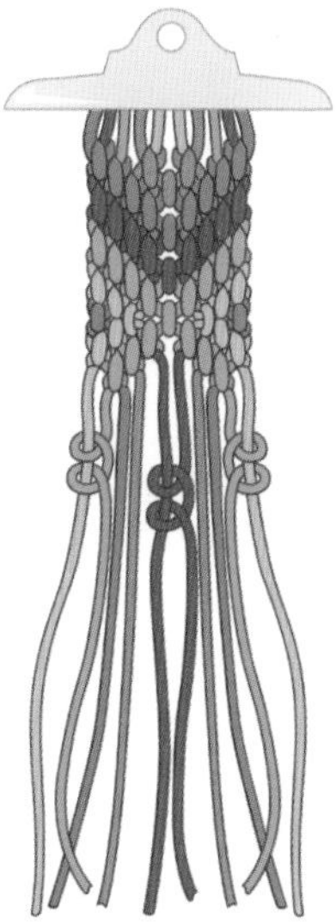

9

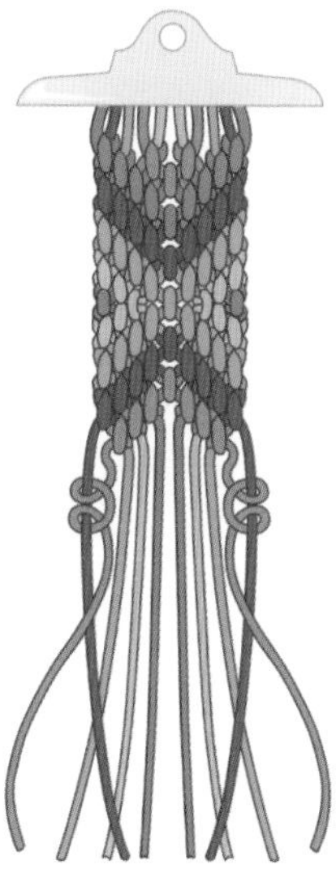

10

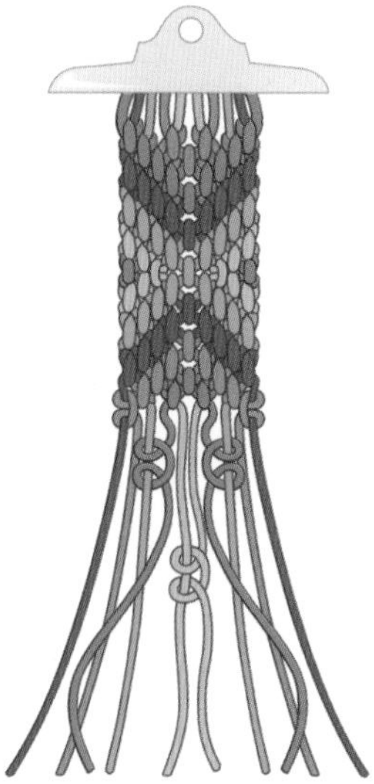

11

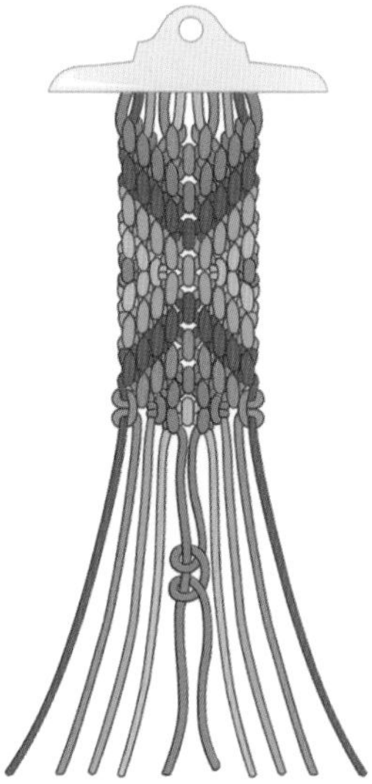

12

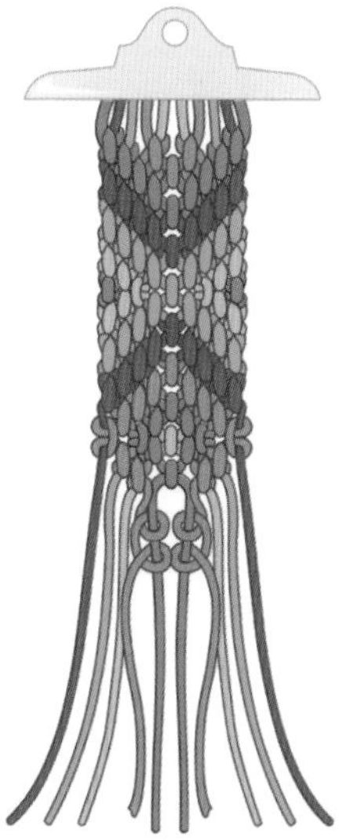

13

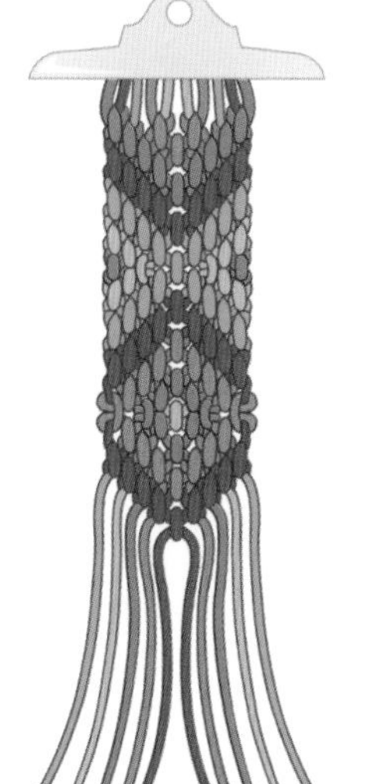

14

Steps 1–14: Follow the instructions for the Diamond/Chevron Combination pattern shown on page 34 to make a bracelet long enough to fit your wrist. The bracelet is formed with five colors: blue, red, green, white, and orange. When the bracelet is finished to the desired length, divide the threads into two sections. Braid the ends to form ties to fasten through the loop at the other end of the bracelet. Knot the ends and trim off the excess thread.

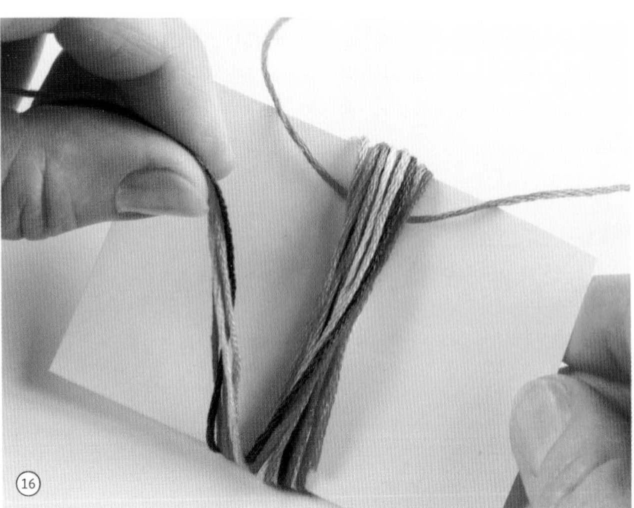

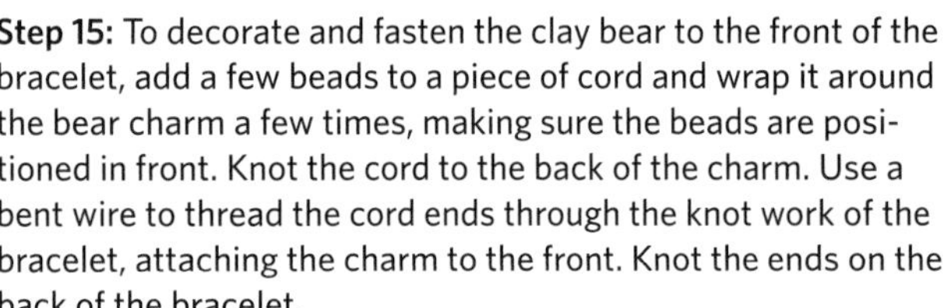
Step 15: To decorate and fasten the clay bear to the front of the bracelet, add a few beads to a piece of cord and wrap it around the bear charm a few times, making sure the beads are positioned in front. Knot the cord to the back of the charm. Use a bent wire to thread the cord ends through the knot work of the bracelet, attaching the charm to the front. Knot the ends on the back of the bracelet.

Step 16: To make a tassel to decorate the bracelet, cut a small piece of cardboard to wrap the threads around. The width of the cardboard will determine the overall length of the tassel. Slip one small piece of loose thread horizontally across the cardboard. This will be used to gather and tie all of the threads together at the top of the tassel after wrapping. Wrap threads over the loose thread and cardboard, wrapping three or more times depending on the desired fullness of the tassel.

Step 17: Slide the cardboard out from the threads and tie the loose thread to gather the threads to form the top of the tassel.

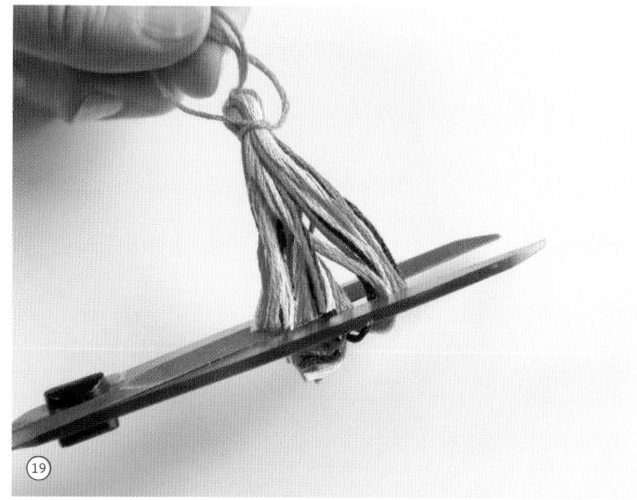

Step 18: Tie another small piece of thread around the group of threads with a knot near the top of the tassel.

Step 19: Trim the ends of the threads to finish the tassel.

Step 20: To attach the tassel to the bracelet, thread the loose thread at the top of the tassel through the knot work of the bracelet and tie an overhand knot on the back. Work the ends of the threads into the knot work of the bracelet to hide them. Clip off the excess thread.
To add a feather accent, coat the end of the feather with white glue. Wrap thread around the wet glue to attach the thread to the feather. Let the glue dry. Attach the feather to the bracelet by stringing the thread through the knot work and then tying a knot on the back of the bracelet. Work the threads into the knots to hide and clip off the excess threads.

Folklorica

The art of enameling is one method used to add color to metal. Glass enamel is applied to metal as a fine glass powder that melts and becomes fused to the metal when heat is applied. By mixing liquid polymer clay with pigments, you can coat the surface of any type of metal and bake the liquid clay onto the surface; this will replicate the look of real glass enamel. For an extra glossy glass finish, coat with a layer of gloss varnish after baking.

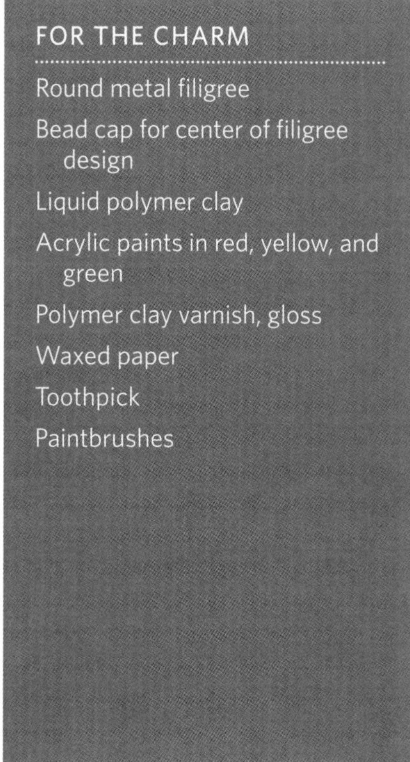

FOR THE CHARM

- Round metal filigree
- Bead cap for center of filigree design
- Liquid polymer clay
- Acrylic paints in red, yellow, and green
- Polymer clay varnish, gloss
- Waxed paper
- Toothpick
- Paintbrushes

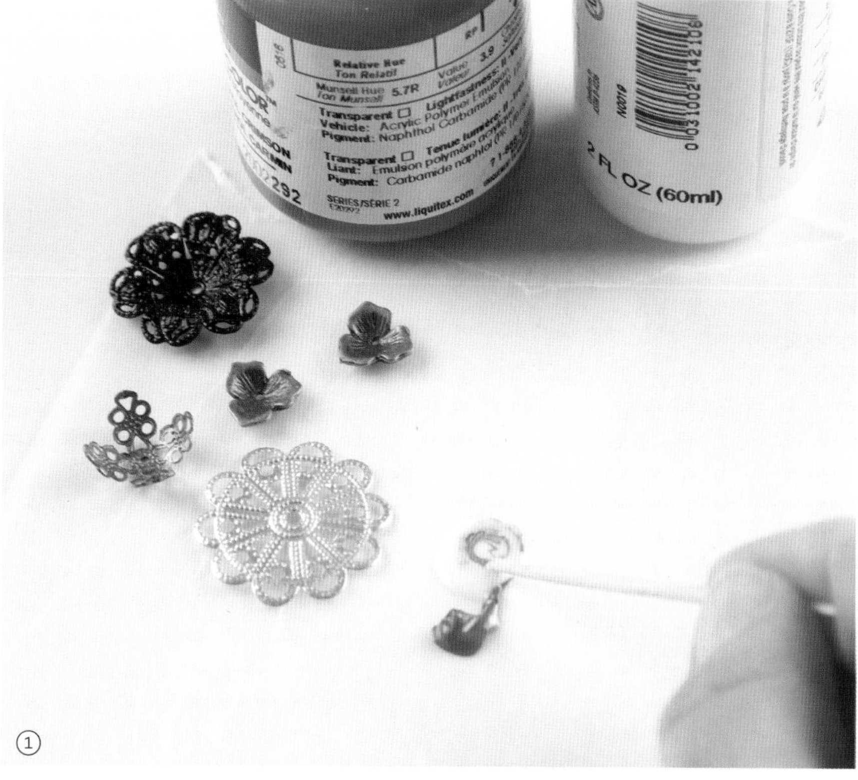

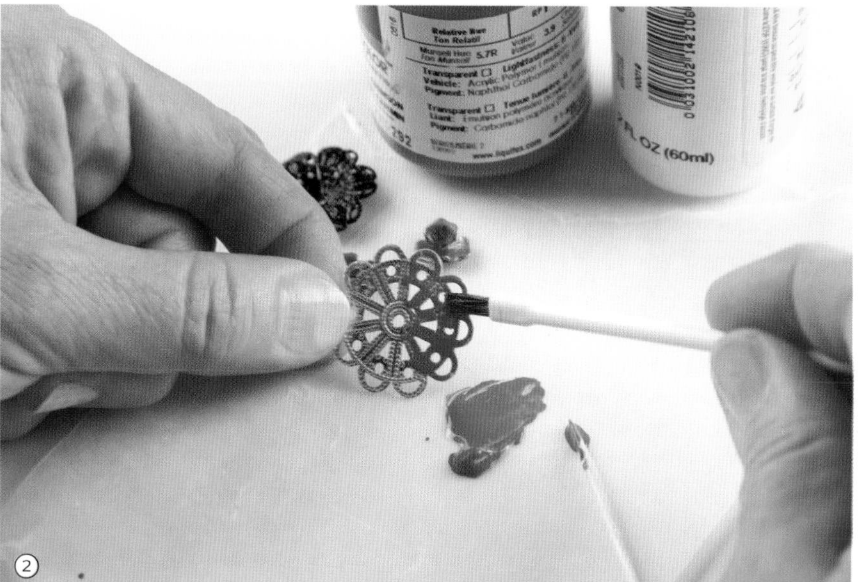

Step 1: On a sheet of waxed paper, mix a drop of acrylic paint into a small pool of liquid polymer, using a toothpick to combine.

Step 2: Apply the mixed liquid polymer clay onto the surface of the metal filigree with a paintbrush. Repeat the same process using another color to paint the inside of a metal bead cap. Bake both pieces according to the manufacturer's instructions. To add shine after baking, you can coat the surface of both pieces with a polymer varnish.

FOR THE BRACELET

- Nylon bead cord (4 pieces, each cut to 50 inches [127 cm])
- Small brass beads
- 4 brass beads
- Crystal bead
- Scissors
- Quick setting two part epoxy resin
- Toothpick
- Waxed paper

HINT *If you would like to make the bracelet adjustable, follow the instructions on page 41 to make a square knot slide.*

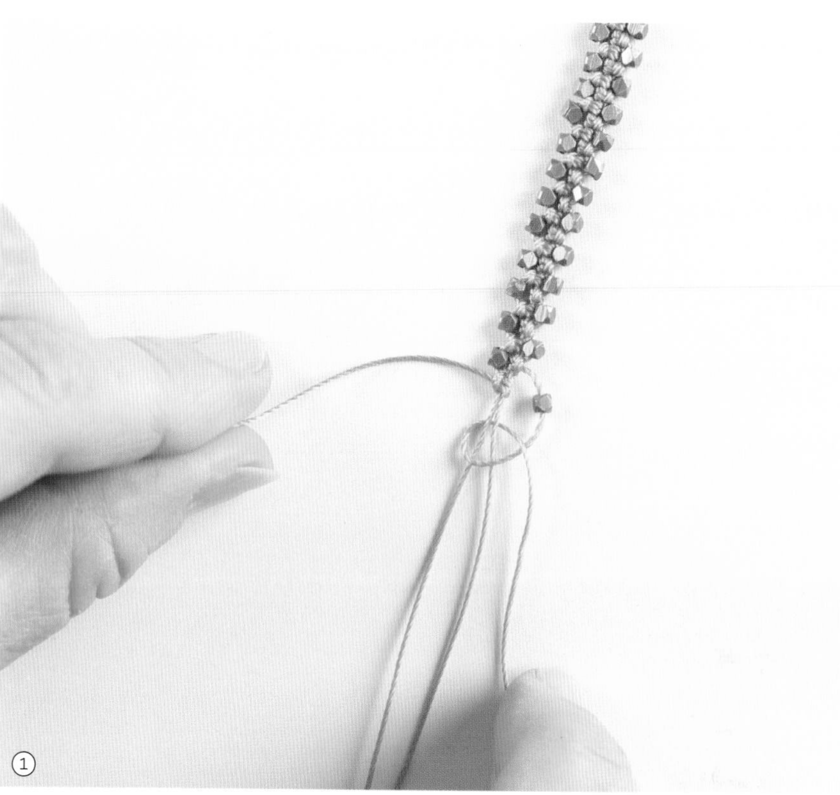

Step 1: To form the bracelet, fold each of the four cords in half and attach two to each side of the filigree with a lark's head knot. You will now have four equal cords at each side of the filigree. Start on one side of the filigree. Leave two cords in the center for the core and then tie one complete square knot over the core using the other two cords. Form the rest of the pattern by tying alternating lark's head knots as shown on page 31, adding a bead on each side after each knot. Secure each bead with a knot underneath as shown in the photo. Repeat the same knot pattern to complete both sides of the bracelet. Finish with an overhand knot with all of the cords on each side. Leave loose ends for tying the bracelet. Embellish the ends of the cords with brass beads and overhand knots. Trim off the excess cord.

Step 2: Add the bead cap with a crystal bead to the center of the filigree. Thread a small piece of cord through the crystal bead, threading both ends through the bead cap. Bring both ends of the cord through the filigree and tie a knot on the back to secure. Use a small amount of epoxy resin to cover and secure the knot on the back of the filigree.

Marigold

A single metal filigree bead is featured in this design. Metal filigree beads can be purchased at bead stores or by searching online. Paint a thin layer of tinted liquid polymer on the bead if you want some of the metal to shine through. For an opaque finish, apply a thicker coating of liquid polymer clay mixed with paint. In this project, cord was selected to match the color of the opaque filigree bead for a simple monochromatic design.

FOR THE BEAD

- Metal filigree beads
- Liquid polymer clay
- Acrylic paint
- Paintbrushes
- Polymer clay varnish
- Wire

FOR THE BRACELET

- Two nylon bead cords, cut one piece 60 inches (152.5 cm) and one piece 30 inches (76 cm)
- Two rhinestone beads
- Two small brass beads

MAKING THE BEAD

Follow the instructions for the Folklorica bracelet on page 129 to coat a metal filigree bead with liquid polymer clay tinted with acrylic paint. Suspend the bead on a wire and bake according to the manufacturer's instructions. After baking, coat with a layer of polymer clay varnish for extra shine.

KNOTTING THE BRACELET

Step 1: Measure down 15 inches (38 cm) on both cords to begin. Make a lark's head loop to start the bracelet by tying the longer cord over the shorter one with a series of lark's head knots as shown on page 39. The longest cord will be used to tie spiral knots to form the pattern. The three shorter cords will serve as the core. To form the bracelet pattern, use the long cord to begin tying a series of spiral half-hitch knots over the core cords. When you reach the mid point of the bracelet, tie a square knot using two of the cords over the other two. Add a rhinestone bead, the filigree bead, and another rhinestone bead. Tie another square knot next to the beads.

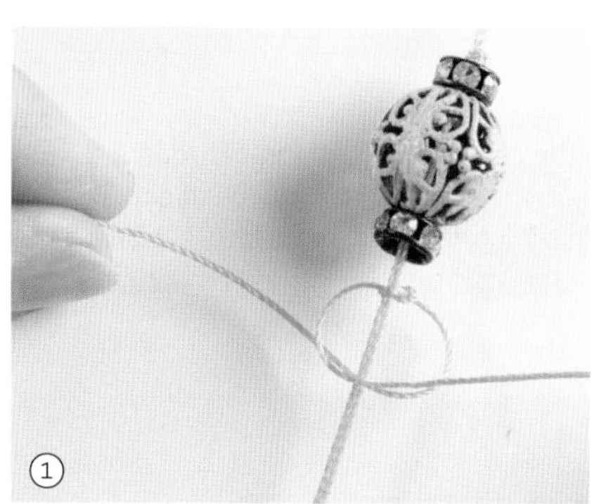

Step 2: Take the longer cord and tie spiral half-hitch knots as you did previously until the bracelet is long enough to fit your wrist. End with an overhand knot. Divide the cords into two sections of two cords each, adding one bead over both cords on each side. End with an overhand knot to secure the beads.

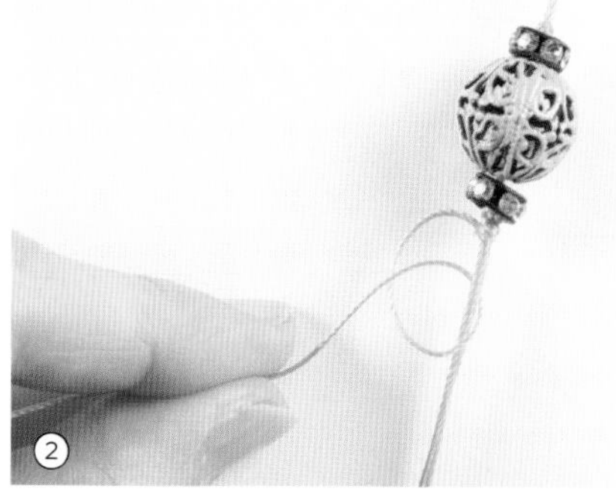

Candy Striper

Want a sugar rush? Wear candy baubles around on your wrist. These beads look good enough to eat. With traditional confectionary colors including pink, red, black, and white, these beads are reminiscent of vintage sweets or the iconic striped awning often associated with an old-fashioned candy shop. Candy inspired beads are made using caning techniques with polymer clay. Eyelets add a nice detail for the holes, allowing the beads to slide freely over a braided cord.

FOR THE BEADS

Polymer clay in white, pink, red, and black

Eyelets

Craft knife or mat cutter blade

Needle tool

①

②

③

④

Step 1: To make a cane, start by stacking sheets of various colors of clay (this photo shows a simple red and white stack). Feed the individual clay layers through a pasta roller to make varied thicknesses. Stack thick layers with thin layers, alternating colors. Use a craft knife or mat cutter blade to slice layers from the stack and wrap the slices around a white log of clay. Let the log rest before rolling. When the clay is firm, roll the clay into a cane until the cane is the right diameter for a bead. Use the knife or blade to slice off sections from the cane to make beads.

Step 2: Pinch the ends of each bead section to form round beads.

Step 3: Press an eyelet onto both sides of the bead and then pierce through the eyelets to align them and to remove the excess clay. Bake the beads.

Step 4: Make more beads made from canes with various candy themed colors.

FOR THE BRACELET

Two pieces nylon bead cord, cut 50 inches (127 cm) each

Glass beads

Rhinestone beads

Lobster claw clasp

Thread burner tool or glue

Step 1: Fold the cords in half. To make the loop, use one of the threads to tie a series of lark's head knots over the other thread, which will serve as the core. Tie enough knots to make a small loop. See page 39 for how to tie a lark's head loop. Form the loop and tie a square knot under the loop.

Step 2: Form the length of the bracelet by tying a four-strand braid; see page 26 for directions. Thread the clay beads with a few glass or rhinestone beads onto the braided cord. Tie a lobster claw clasp to the end of the cord with a knot. Clip off the excess cord and seal the knot with a thread burner tool or with glue.

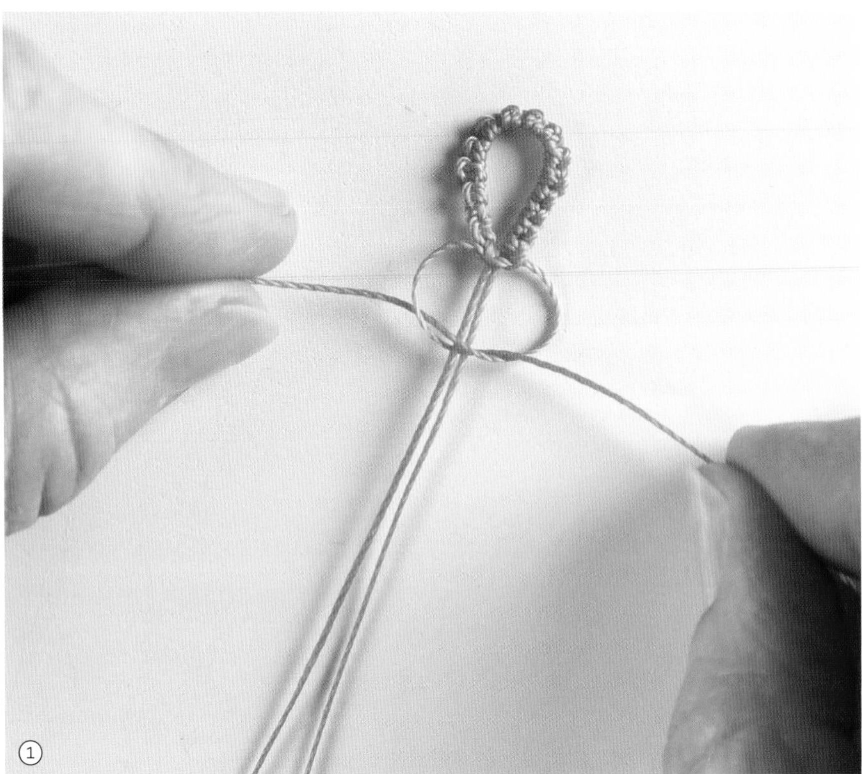

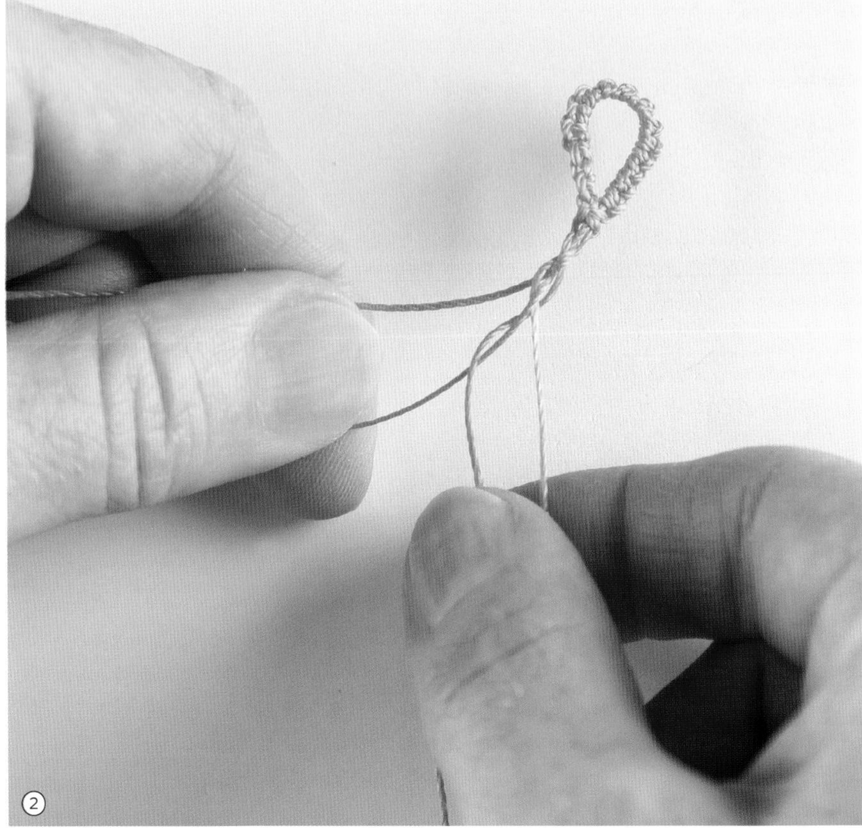

VARIATION

Peppermint Twist

Several techniques are used to turn red and white polymer clay into fanciful candy cane, peppermint star, and licorice twist beads. The secret to making neat canes for these beads is to let the clay rest between steps. A firm type of polymer clay works best for this project.

FOR THE BEADS

- Red and white polymer clay
- Eyelets
- Craft knife or mat cutter blade
- Glass beads

FOR THE BRACELET

- Two pieces red nylon bead cord, cut to 50 inches (127 cm) lengths
- Lobster claw clasp
- Needle tool

MAKING THE BEAD

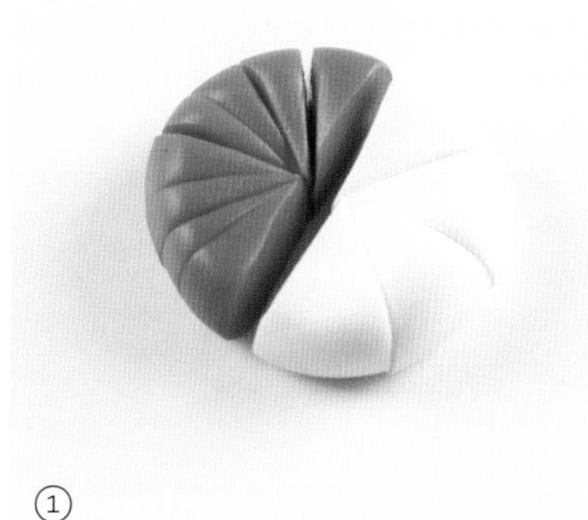

①

Step 1: Roll a ball of white clay and another ball the same size of red clay. Flatten each ball to make a circle. Use a sharp blade to cut the white clay circle into eight wedges and the red clay circle into sixteen wedges. This photo shows how the wedges are cut like slices of a cake or pie.

Step 2: Assemble the wedges into a circle by alternating six white wedges with six red wedges. Press them tightly together and let the clay rest to firm up.

②

Step 3: After the clay is firm, turn the circle of wedges on its side and roll it into a cane until the desired bead diameter is reached. Use a craft knife or mat cutter blade to slice off sections to form the peppermint beads.

Step 4: Pinch around the edges of the beads slightly to taper. Use a needle tool to pierce a hole for stringing through the side of the bead.

Step 5: To make a red licorice twist, roll out a long rectangle shape of red clay. Let the clay rest to firm up. Twist the rectangle to resemble a licorice twist candy. Cut the twist into small sections to use as beads. Pierce a hole through the length of the bead before baking according to the manufacturer's instructions.

KNOTTING THE BRACELET

Thread all of the baked beads onto a four-strand braided cord as shown for the Candy Striper bracelet on page 134.

Rawhide

Polymer clay has a similar matte finish and flexible texture that resembles leather. Mix a shade of clay to match any color of leather and use leather stamping tools to texture the clay. For variety, use black or red clay to make the faux leather. For a dark leather color like black, use white paint instead of brown to emphasize the details.

MAKING THE CHARM

FOR THE CHARM

- Brown polymer clay (or any other leather color)
- Leather stamping tools
- Needle tool
- Ceramic mug for baking
- Craft knife
- Paintbrush
- Antiquing medium or dark brown acrylic paint
- Paper towel

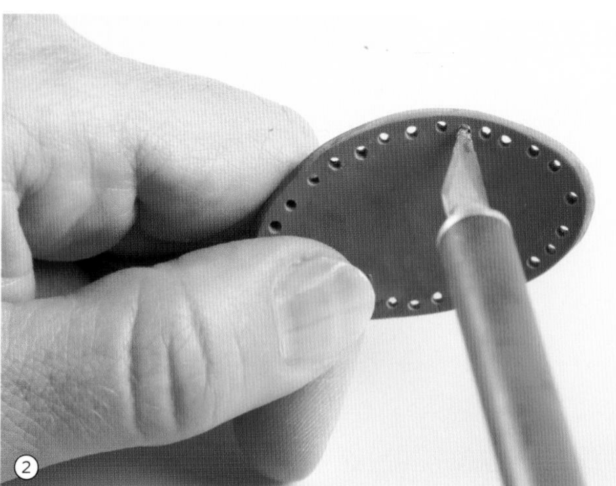

Step 1: Roll out a sheet of brown clay on the thickest setting of the pasta roller, or roll a thick sheet by hand. Cut the sheet into an oval shape to make the bracelet centerpiece. Stamp textures into the clay with leather stamps. Drape the shape over a ceramic mug to form a curve while baking. Use a needle tool to pierce holes around the edge of the clay centerpiece. The holes will be refined later.

Step 2: Bake the clay over a ceramic mug. After baking, use the tip of a craft knife to refine and enlarge the holes around the edge of the piece. To do this, gently twirl the tip of the knife through the pilot hole to shave the clay away. Darken the recessed areas of the textures with antiquing medium or acrylic paint. Wipe off the excess with a damp paper towel.

KNOTTING THE BRACELET

FOR THE BRACELET

- Two 50 inch (127 cm) lengths of white nylon bead cord
- Four 40 inch (101.5 cm) lengths of white nylon bead cord
- Wire for threading cord
- Silver beads

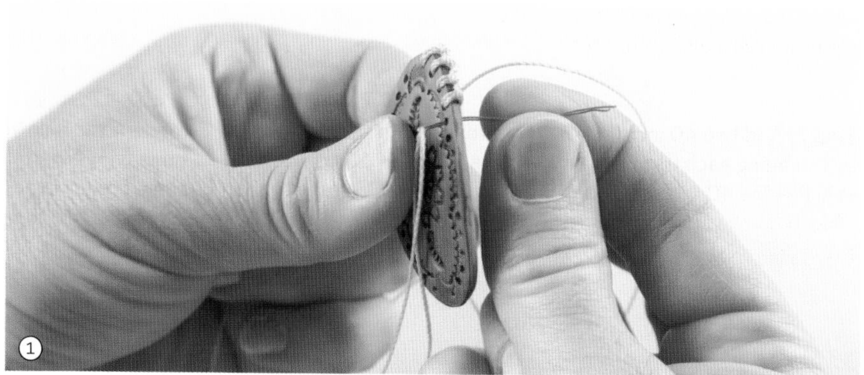

Step 1: Measure down about 20 inches (51 cm) on one of the 50 inch (127 cm) cords. With the longer end, start on one side of the oval and tie lark's head knots around the long edge of the piece, working a full lark's head knot through each hole. Use a bent wire to thread the cord through the holes. When the lark's head knots have been completed around one long side of the oval, the two loose cords at each end will measure about 20 inches (51 cm) each. With the other 50 inch (127 cm) cord, repeat the same design along the opposite side of the oval.

Step 2: Add two 40 inch (101.5 cm) cords to each side of the oval by threading each through the holes the 50 inch (127 cm) cords exit. Pull the 40 inch (101.5 cm) cords to the middle, resulting in 20 inch (51 cm) cords. There will be six cords hanging from each side of the oval.

Step 3: The bracelet is formed with an alternating square knot pattern. See page 28. Start on one side of the oval and tie two square knots side by side, using three cords each as shown.

Step 4: Tie a single square knot in the middle of the next row using four cords.

Step 5: For the next row, tie two square knots side by side as in step 3. Add a silver bead to the two central cords under the knots. The bead is added in place of a single square knot for this row. For the following row, tie two square knots side by side. Continue tying a pattern of alternating square knots. Add a bead in place of the single square knot after every third single knot in the pattern. Or add more beads if desired. Finish the other side and tie an overhand knot to secure the cords. Leave the tails free to tie on the bracelet or add an adjustable square knot slide closure as shown on page 41. Divide the cord tails into two strands on each side and add beads with overhand knots to the ends.

Resources

POLYMER CLAY, LIQUID POLYMER CLAY, POLYMER VARNISHES, POLYMER TOOLS, AND SUPPLIES

Clay Factory Inc.
www.clayfactory.net
Cernit brand polymer clay and other brands of polymer clay, tools, and supplies

Cool Tools
www.cooltools.us
Jewelry making tools, stamps, and textures

Kato Polyclay
www.katopolyclay.com
Polymer clay, liquid polymer clay, and supplies

KemperTools
www.kempertools.com
Pattern cutters

Metal Clay Supply
www.metalclaysupply.com
Clay sculpting tools, molds, and clay cutters

Polymer Clay Express
www.polymerclayexpress.com
Polymer clay, polymer cutters, tools, and supplies

Sculpey
www.sculpey.com
Polymer clay, polymer clay varnish, and supplies

Staedtler
www.staedtler.com/en
FIMO modeling clay, polymer clay varnish, and metallic powders

Viva Decor
www.viva-decor.de
Pardo polymer clay and supplies

THREAD AND CORD

beadshop.com
www.beadshop.com
Nylon cord and beading supplies

Caravan Beads
www.caravanbeads.net
Nylon cord and beading supplies

DMC, USA
www.dmc-usa.com
DMC cotton embroidery floss and other thread types including metallic—DMC products are available in most craft- and fabric-supply stores.

Fusion Beads
www.fushionbeads.com
Nylon cord and beading supplies

Jewels in Fiber
www.store.jewelsinfiber.com
Nylon cord and beading supplies

Tinsel Trading Company
www.tinseltrading.com
Metallic threads and vintage and unique stringing materials

BEADING SUPPLIERS

Dynasty Art Studio
www.dynastyartstudio.com
Rubber stamps and texture sheets
Thread and nylon beading cord
Beads and supplies
Dichroic glass dots

Euro Tool
www.eurotool.com
Jewelry-making tools

FDJ on Time
www.fdjtool.com
Jewelry-making tools and beading supplies

Fire Mountain Gems and Beads
www.firemountaingems.com
Tools, cord, beads, and jewelry-making supplies

Rio Grande
www.riogrande.com
Beads and stringing supplies
Baroque Art® Gilders Paste
Pliers and jewelry-making tools
Belicold Silicone Mold Rubber Compound

Shipwreck Beads
www.shipwreckbeads.com
Tools, cord, beads, and jewelry-making supplies

The Beadsmith
www.helby.com (wholesale only, search site for retailers)
Thread Zap II (thread burner tool)

GENERAL CRAFT SUPPLIES AND JEWELRY-MAKING PRODUCTS

D. Blumchen & Company, Inc.
www.blumchen.com
Dresden paper die-cuts (foil wings)

Hobby Lobby
www.hobbylobby.com
Beading, jewelry-making supplies, embroidery floss, and art mediums such as paint

Jo-Ann Fabric and Craft Store
www.joann.com
Beading, jewelry-making supplies, embroidery floss, and art mediums such as paint

Michaels
www.michaels.com
Beading, jewelry-making supplies, embroidery floss, and art mediums such as paint

National Artcraft
www.nationalartcraft.com
Rub-on Metallic Highlights
Rhinestone Chain

Sherri Haab Designs
www.sherrihaab.com
ITS Image Transfer Medium and ITS paper

Tandy Leather
www.tandyleatherfactory.com
Leather-stamping tools

PAINT, PIGMENTS, INK, AND OTHER ART MEDIUMS

Ebay
www.ebay.com
Beading supplies, filigree, and jewelry-making supplies

Etsy
www.etsy.com
Unique beading supplies, filigree, vintage images

Jacquard Products
www.jacquardproducts.com
Piñata alcohol inks
Pearl Ex pigment powders

Liquitex
www.liquitex.com
Acrylic paints, metallic paint, and acrylic mediums

Plaid
www.plaidonline.com
FolkArt ® Mediums, antiquing medium, and acrylic paint

Prismacolor
www.prismacolor.com
Colored pencils and art markers

Ranger Ink
www.rangerink.com
Adirondack® alcohol inks

MOLD MAKING SUPPLIES

Alumilite Corporation
www.alumlite.com
Amazing mold putty and silicone mold-making materials

Environmental Technologies Inc.
www.eti-usa.com
Silicone mold-making materials
Granite powders

Smooth-On
www.smooth-on.com
Silicone mold-making materials

About the Author

SHERRI HAAB is an award-winning, bestselling craft book author, with more than twenty-five books published to date. She has several DVDs and has appeared on many television networks including HGTV, DIY, JTV, PBS, and local programs. As a certified metal clay instructor, she leads numerous craft and jewelry-making workshops internationally. With her talent for trend spotting and product development, she is an innovator in the craft industry known worldwide. Her work includes books for children and adults and her own line of craft supplies. She and her husband, Dan, live in Saratoga Spring, Utah. www.sherrihaab.com

Index